MW00427299

The Prayer Habit

A 40 Day Devotional

Anika Jones

The Prayer Habit

Copyright © 2019 by Anika Jones

All rights reserved. This book or any portion thereof may not be reproduced or used in any manner whatsoever without the express written permission of the author except for the use of brief quotations in a book review.

Request for permission should be submitted in writing via email to anikajones1@gmail.com.

Scripture quotations marked (NLT) are taken from the Holy Bible, New Living Translation, copyright © 1996, 2004, 2007, 2013, 2015 by Tyndale House Foundation. Used by permission of Tyndale House Publishers, Inc., Carol Stream, Illinois 60188. All rights reserved.

Scriptures marked NIV are taken from the NEW INTERNATIONAL VERSION (NIV): Scripture taken from THE HOLY BIBLE, NEW INTERNATIONAL VERSION ®. Copyright© 1973, 1978, 1984, 2011 by Biblica, Inc.™. Used by permission of Zondervan.

Scriptures marked NKJV are taken from the NEW KING JAMES VERSION (NKJV): Scripture taken from the NEW KING JAMES VERSION®. Copyright© 1982 by Thomas Nelson, Inc. Used by permission. All rights reserved.

This book is dedicated to my grandmother,

one of the greatest prayer warriors I know.

To Mama-

You never kept your prayer habit a secret-- and for that, I am grateful! I watch you live your life with such intention and urgency because you know there is more to come. It is a known fact that your long-standing custom is to have a prayer meeting with anyone who comes to visit you. You sing a few hymns, read from the Bible, exhort us and then pray with such spiritual intelligence. As a child, I found your prayer habit to be annoying. I didn't understand and could not appreciate the greatest legacy you could pass on-- an unwavering faith in God! Well, your prayer habit is contagious because here I am at 41, praying for a double portion of what you possess. I've watched you all these years cultivate a profound intimacy with God, inspiring me to go deeper. You are one of the strongest women I know. Sure, your 92 years of living has caused your body to become frail, but with the passing of time, your faith in God has become even stronger. What an example you are. You shared with me on multiple occasions how the Lord told you He would multiply your blessings and your response was, "Not natural blessings but spiritual blessings, Lord." The Lord knew your desire was not for material gain but for your family members to be saved. He heard your request, Mama, and He gave you a loud yes! This book is just one of the many proofs! I know that until you breathe your last breath, prayer will continue to be your habit. Thank you for such a great legacy.

Love you,
Anika

Foreword

In everyone's life, there should be books that make you reevaluate where you are in life at a given point. This book, **The Prayer Habit: 40 Day Devotional,** is definitely one of those books that helps in having an effective prayer life.

This book clearly outlines the process required to authenticate one's prayer life. Anika Jones has transparently poured out her heart into helping every reader develop a healthy, sober, and consistent prayer life predicated on Godly truths and deep introspection of one's own limitations and strengths.

Not being an emotional person by nature, it was very difficult for me to develop intimacy with God as a father. However, after reading this book, I can say that Anika has outlined simplistic ways to connect with our heavenly father in a more meaningful way that helped me improve on my intimacy with God.

In my private times of prayer, I had become a "professional" intercessor, weak on being transparent and garnering a relationship with God that makes me fall in love with Him on the level described in this book.

After reading this book, I now know from a credible source and personal experience, how "easy" it is to just "talk" to God. I know there is more fruit that the readers of this book will gain if they follow the processes outlined and be consistent in simply "talking to God". I declare that the readers of this book will have an insatiable desire to commune with God daily in order to develop the intimacy that God desires of His children; and also that the effects will be farther reaching than anything you could have imagined and impacting for generations to come.

Terralyn Frazier, Teacher (M.Ed. Reading) and Intercessor
Women Of Restoration and Deliverance (W.O.R.D.)
W.O.R.D. Prayer Group Organizer
W.O.R.D.prayerline@gmail.com

Acknowledgments

I am so giddy with excitement to know that this project went from a good idea to become a published book. I am so grateful for those who helped to make it a reality.

-To my friend Terralyn Frazier, I am overwhelmed with gratitude when I think about your willingness to take time out of your busy schedule to edit this book. You are so good at what you do! Your attention to detail and understanding of the word was exactly what I needed. All of your suggestions and corrections are appreciated. Thank you!

-To my sister Tamara Stewart-Hadaway, thank for taking time out of your schedule to provide editing feedback. I loved the way you asked me questions without giving me the answers, it helped me to think about what I really wanted to say.

-To my friend Keegan Harkins, you have been a huge source of encouragement for me in my writing journey. You kept me accountable and provided the encouragement I needed to keep going. You never made me feel bad about asking many questions. You kept me from falling apart and giving up when I didn't understand the technical side of self-publishing. Your patience and desire to see others thrive in their gift is refreshing.

-To my six children, you are all so precious. My deepest desire is for each of you to develop a prayer habit. I love you more than words can express.

-Finally, to my husband, Tyrone, I love the way you support me in doing what God has called me to do. What a gift you have been to me. In so many ways, you have been one of my favorite answered prayers. I love you!

Contents

Dear Reader,

Those who know me well, know that I can talk. Before I came to Christ, I spent a lot of time talking and listening to everyone else *but* God. Sure, I did my occasional insincere prayers when I wanted to get out of a bind or needed a favor, but a true prayer life? Definitely lacking. That was problematic and I have the stories to prove it. But when I came to Christ, I naturally fell in love with prayer. I loved talking to Him and having Him respond. I consider my ability to pray to the Creator of the Universe as one of my greatest treasures. For me, prayer is not a chore; it is a privilege.

My heart aches when I speak to individuals who abandon the thing that is their lifeline...prayer. I see people living their lives running around in circles because they refuse to maintain communication with God. Some may have a faulty view of prayer for various reasons, including, but not limited to the following rationale:

- They complicate prayer by assuming it has to be a grand production.

- They think if they cannot pray like the individual they respect, then it is not real prayer.

- They avoid prayer because they think they don't have the 'right' words to say.

- They think they should pray only when they feel like it.

- They feel that real, consistent prayer is reserved for those in church leadership.

- They feel unworthy and assume God does not want to hear from them.

And the list goes on.

Despite each person's reservation, I have great news, God invites us all to pray-- The introvert, the extrovert, the midvert (did I just create a word?). In Matthew 27:51, the veil in the temple was torn in two during Jesus' crucifixion, symbolic of the access we now have to go boldly before God. Therefore, I can pray anywhere and anytime; and that is exactly what God invites us to do.

On the pages of this book are parts of my heart; sounds melodramatic I know, but it's true. I share with you lessons I have learned about prayer, intending to encourage you to form a prayer habit. I invite you to read one entry each day and take the time to answer the reflection questions and meditate on the scriptures for reflection. At the end of each entry is a prayer starter. However, I do not intend for this to be the only prayer you pray for the day. Instead, use it to provoke you to pray and build from the words on the pages.

Who exactly is this book for? It's for the one who doesn't feel worthy to pray. It is for the one who can't find the right words to pray. It is for the one who once had a vibrant prayer life but got distracted and trying to find their way back to that secret place. It is for the one who still loves to pray.

Are you ready for this forty-day journey? Let us begin!

When Prayer Is Your Habit

When prayer is your habit...
You expect it to uproot mountains and for giants to fall.
The supernatural becomes your norm.

When prayer is your habit...
You know there is nothing too hard for God,
So, you cling to His promises no matter how long.

When prayer is your habit...
You forgive seventy times seven,
Not allowing offenses to keep you out of heaven.

When prayer is your habit...
You gain peace beyond your understanding,
Not easily moved by external circumstances.

When prayer is your habit...
You are confident it will all work together for your good,
including suffering,
So even during the pain, you offer prayers of
thanksgiving.

When prayer is your habit...
You don't fear death, knowing it is not the end,
Because being in Christ means you are living to live again!

When prayer is your habit...
You no longer yearn for what doesn't satisfy,
You instead feast on Jesus, the bread of life.

Day 1: Prayer and Studying God's Word

We can find the will of God in His word which is why studying it is helpful to have an effective prayer life. Don't just read the word of God, take the time to study it and when you do, the word of God will read you. Allow the word to turn the pages of your heart and reveal the areas that need a spiritual makeover. We are being perfected so there is always something to work on. We rush through reading the bible and instead of having a bible study we have a quick drive-by bible reading. We then lament that we are in the word, but we are not seeing any change. Could it be that we just need to slow down and digest what we read? Could it be that we need to take the time to meditate and answer questions that allow us to connect with the material before us? When I was in school, for me to grasp the material, I had to read it more than once. I took the time to look up words in the dictionary to ensure I understood what I was reading. I highlighted certain sentences; I jotted down notes to summarize what I just read in my own words. Whenever I took this approach and it was time for the test, I did well. Why? Because I took the time to study the material instead of just reading it, so the material was in me. I try to take the same approach when I study the word of God.

Below are a few practical ways I study the word of God.

- I dedicate time daily to study God's word. I don't wait for it to happen. I try to be intentional about having a specific time for bible study.

- I pick a specific scripture that addresses an area that I need to work on. For example, I have been studying Proverbs 29:25 because I have had an on and off relationship with the fear of man. Proverbs 29:25 says, "Fearing people is a dangerous trap, but trusting the LORD means safety." For the first few days of my study, I focused only on that verse and allowed the Lord to speak to me. I looked up the verse in different translations.

- After a few days, I googled this exact phrase, "cross-references for Proverbs 29:25." This search led me to many scriptures that carry the same theme as Proverbs 29:25. I chose a few of those scriptures and read them over the course of two weeks. I took my time to digest them. I highlighted key phrases, I took notes, and I sat and reflected on what I read. I prayed prayers connected to those scriptures.

- At the end of the two weeks, I took some time to jot down all I learned. I did not open my bible to gather the information; I wrote what I remembered on my own. I then asked myself the following questions for this study, "What are my symptoms, how do I fear man? I took some time to reflect on my areas of struggle and wrote honest answers to these questions.

- I concluded this study by praying for deliverance from the specific things I wrote. I suspect that this will be more than a one-time prayer.

As you seek to develop a prayer habit, I encourage you to slow down and spend time studying the word of God. It will greatly impact your prayer life.

Scripture for Meditation:

Psalm 119:11 (NLT)

I have hidden your word in my heart, that I might not sin against you.

Prayer Starter:

God, help me to make studying your word a priority...

Reflection Questions:

Do you just read the word, or do you actually make time to study it?

How often do you study the word of God?

Do you notice a difference in your prayer life when you make time to study God's word?

Day 2: Know Who You Are Praying To

The Lord's Prayer is something that many are familiar with. I encourage you to memorize this passage of scripture; but it is even more important to use it as a template for how we should pray. Beyond reciting it verbatim, this prayer is more powerful when we make it personal and fill in the blanks with our own circumstances. This passage came right after Jesus tells the people some things to avoid in prayer in Mathew 6:5-8. Things such as making a public spectacle when praying or constant repetition and much speaking to sound impressive. Instead, He says, In Mathew 6:9 "This, then, is how you should pray: "'Our Father in heaven...'"

To pray effectively, we must first know who we are praying to. This opening sets the tone for prayer. I base my level of transparency in a conversation on the depth of the relationship to whom I'm speaking with. Do you know who you are speaking to in prayer?

Galatians 4:4-7 reminds us we are no longer slaves, but we are now sons and daughters of God, and call Him Abba. It shocked the Jews that Jesus would use such a term as Abba which means daddy when describing God; they thought it irreverent. Take a deep breath and relax, you are talking to your daddy; you are not praying to some distant God. This should shift our approach and bring a level of comfort and confidence and not one of performance. This was such a hard concept for me to grasp when I first came to the Lord. With time, God had to show me that my rigor was not His biggest concern. He was more focused on having a relationship with me; he was my daddy. He is not looking for my rigor, but my affection.

My prayers will be routine and ineffective if I approach it like a business call, as opposed to an intimate conversation with my daddy. There are no formalities needed. There is no need to make sure my grammar is correct or to make sure I have well phrased speeches. Sometimes we approach prayer as if we are talking to a jail warden that is ready to whip us in order; as opposed to a loving daddy who wants to heal, restore, and redeem us. The more I commune with my daddy, the more I want to come back.

Scripture for Meditation:

Galatians 4:4-7 (NLT)

But when the right time came, God sent his Son, born of a woman, subject to the law. God sent him to buy freedom for us who were slaves to the law, so that he could adopt us as his very own children. And because we are his children, God has sent the Spirit of his Son into our hearts, prompting us to call out, "Abba, Father." Now you are no longer a slave but God's own child. And since you are his child, God has made you his heir.

Prayer Starter:

Dear God, please help me relax in your presence and understand that you desire intimacy with me in prayer. Help me know that you delight in having me come to speak with you and that you are not looking for a performance. Father, show me the root of my hesitancy to view you as daddy and not a distant God...

Reflection Questions:

What is your prevalent view on God the father?

Do you see Him as a distant father waiting to punish you if you mess up?

Do you feel uptight and focus on making sure you have the right presentation as if it were a business meeting? Or do you view Him as a loving God inviting you to commune with Him?

How has your perspective of Him impacted your prayer life?

Day 3: Petition Him

In Matthew 6:11, Jesus teaches that I am to ask God to provide my daily bread. My daily bread is not limited to my natural needs such as finances to put food on the table and to pay my bills. Sometimes my daily bread is peace of mind, and stability in my emotions. Some are fiercely independent and think it is unnecessary to ask God for what they need. In our culture, we applaud independence and our ability to work things out and meet our own needs. However, on closer inspection this fierce independence is simply pride on display. From the beginning we have been faced with the temptation to be our own God. This is what happened in Genesis 3, when the devil convinced Adam and Eve that they would be like God if they ate from the tree of the knowledge of good and evil. It was a lie then, and it remains a lie now. We must allow God to be God in our lives and petition Him to meet our needs and not take matters in our own hands.

Some of you, because of unfortunate life circumstances were forced to fend for yourself. You did not have anyone you could trust to provide for you. Consequently, you were conditioned to not ask for help. What a heavy load to carry! Whatever we need, God can provide. He can provide water from a rock (Exodus 17:6) and food in the wilderness (Exodus 16) just like He did for the children of Israel. The beautiful thing about God is that He invites us to pray to Him for our needs. He actually wants to meet them. Our petition for our daily bread is not an annoyance to Him. He delights in providing for His children. He is a good Father! But let us be sure to not be like the children of Israel and scoff at God's provision.

The term "daily bread" lets me know that I must return each day to be filled up. I cannot think the prayer I prayed on Sunday is good enough to carry me all week. In the natural, unless we are fasting, most of us have daily meals and when we don't, we feel the effects. It is also important to note that sometimes we don't know what we really need, what we prioritize as our daily bread will not bring lasting satisfaction. Ultimately what we should petition God for is more of His son. In John 6:35, Jesus refers to Himself as the bread of life. I must come each day to feast on Jesus because when all is said and done, Jesus is all I need. Mathew 6:33 reminds us that we are to first seek the Kingdom of God and all His righteousness and all other things will be added. As we seek to be filled up with Jesus first, every other need will be met. Many go to other sources for their daily bread-jobs, relationships, etc., but only Jesus satisfies. He's the only one that fills up.

Scriptures for Meditation:

John 6:35 (NLT)

Jesus replied, "I am the bread of life. Whoever comes to me will never be hungry again. Whoever believes in me will never be thirsty.

John 6:51 (NLT)

I am the living bread that came down from heaven. Anyone who eats this bread will live forever, and this bread, which I will offer so the world my live, is my flesh.

James 1:17 (NLT)

Whatever is good and perfect comes down to us from God our Father, who created all the lights in the heavens. He never changes or casts a shifting shadow.

Prayer Starter:

Dear God, please expose any pride or hesitancy in my heart that may keep me from coming and asking you for what I need. Help me to understand that you are a good Father who delights in providing for your children...

Reflection Questions:

Is it easy for you to pray and ask God for what you need or is there a block?

Do you view Jesus as your daily bread, do you view Him as enough? Or are you looking to be filled up/satisfied by something or someone else?

Day 4: Hitting the Floor and Dropping the Weight

At the start of a new year, many of us have health goals. We may have a few extra pounds to lose, desire to become toned, or change our eating habits. I often put together an action plan to meet my health goals, however I also implement another method to drop a different weight. I am committed to hitting the floor on my knees in prayer to drop all the weight that is not mine to carry.

Before I pull out my violin and tell you all that's wrong...

Before I run to the pantry for a treat to calm my nerves and give me temporary relief...

Before I get all worked up trying to explain and convince my husband of my point of view...

Before I tell you yes when the answer should be no, but I am looking for your approval...

Before I feel discouraged that I have entered another year and I still have not seen the manifestation of promises I desperately desire...

Before I get burdened with your situation and feel bad that I can't fix it and make it all better...

BEFORE I DO ANY OF THAT... I will drop to the floor and unload that weight in prayer.

Carrying around that extra weight takes a toll on me. I become spiritually bloated and lethargic. And if I don't drop the weight in prayer, it affects my heart. I begin to think and say things that are not in alignment with God's word. So, while I will continue making good health a part of my new

year's resolution, at the top of the list will be to drop a
different kind of weight in prayer.

Scriptures for Meditation:

Psalm 55:22 (NLT)

Give your burdens to the LORD, and he will take
care of you. He will not permit the godly to slip and
fall.

Matthew 11:28 (NLT)

Then Jesus said, "Come to me, all of you who are
weary and carry heavy burdens, and I will give you
rest.

Psalm 95:6-7 (NIV)

Come, let us bow down in worship, let us kneel
before the Lord our Make; for he is our God and we
are the people of his pasture, the flock under his
care.

Prayer Starter:

Dear God, please help me to always turn to you in prayer. Help me not to turn to other things when I feel weighed down...

Reflection Questions:

What weight have you been carrying?

What things are you worrying about?

What things are weighing you down?

Day 5: On My Knees

My floors were gross and in desperate need of cleaning. I passed on using the steam mop and went the old-fashioned route. Out came the bucket and rags as I got on my knees. My intention was to clean JUST the floors. However, being on my knees allowed me to see other areas that also needed to be cleaned... my walls, the legs of the table and chairs, the baseboards and the lower cabinets. I was on my knees a lot longer than intended, but the results were worth it.
Isn't that how it is when we get on our knees in prayer? Admittedly, I have times when I want to quickly blow off steam in prayer and get on with my daily agenda. However, being in the presence of God brings all the "dirty" stuff to the surface. As I commune with Him in sincere prayer, He shows me areas where I have such things as jealousy, bitterness, and pride—areas that need some serious cleansing.

It is not enough to just get on my knees for a moment, but I must stay there longer than intended sometimes. I must enter His presence with thanksgiving and offer true praise, acknowledging who He is and what He has done for me. I have to get comfortable crying out to God, telling Him all, withholding nothing. But it doesn't stop at me sharing, I must have a dialogue and learn when it's His turn to speak during prayer. I must stay on my knees as opposed to running away when He doesn't answer the way I desire.

To get really 'clean,' I cannot rely on a quick "I'm just praying because this is what a Christian is to do" kind of prayer. My life would be no cleaner than my kitchen, showing a surface cleaning. Prayer must be a priority. He is coming back for a church without spot or wrinkle or any other blemish.

Yes, it takes time, but the results are a positively transformed life and greater connection with God. Just like the satisfaction I gained from my housekeeping duties; prayer will also prove to be well worth it.

Prayer is free therapy and you can rest assured that the therapist understands what you are going through; He's been there and came out victorious. It is always convenient to pray, as a matter of fact, 1 Thessalonians 5:17 tells us to pray at all times. God's ears are always open to our cry. When you earnestly pray, it produces great results.

Scripture for Meditation:

James 5:16 (NLT)

The earnest prayer of a righteous person has great power and produces wonderful results.

Prayer Starter:

Dear God, I thank you for your cleansing power and the sanctifying work you are doing with me. Help me yield to the process...

Reflection Questions:

Have you been consistently hitting the floor in prayer or are you content with having drive-by prayers?

Day 6: I Am Going to Tell My Daddy on You

My children excel in telling on each other. There are six, so there are many opportunities for disagreements throughout the course of the day. When things get a little rough, you can hear one of them shouting, "I will tell Daddy/Mommy on you." When they feel they are losing the battle, they give up on arguing and run straight to my husband, Tyrone, or me, to pour out their distress. When they tell on each other, they hold nothing back. They spill their raw emotions and they leave no stone unturned. They are not worried about composure; how it looks or sounds. If the offense is great, there are even real hot crocodile tears.

If only we could take a page out of their book. Instead of fighting and trying to prove our point, defend ourselves, fight our own battles we should run and tell our heavenly father all about it in prayer. At times, they may annoy Tyrone and me with all the telling. Rarely do we invite them to tell us all the nitty gritty, but not so with our Heavenly Father. He lovingly invites us to come. Tell Him all, hold nothing back in prayer.

Cast It. Throw it.

Give all of your worries to Him. Why? He cares for us. Lovingly and perfectly. He cares for me. He cares for you. Don't worry about trying to find the words, just pour it all out to your daddy. Don't hold back the tears, let them flow. Your tears and raw emotions are safe with Him. You can be vulnerable.

After the kids get through telling, we often ask them what their part in the offense was. Be prepared to hear and RECEIVE God's response after you tell on someone else.

God is masterful at showing us ourselves, things we didn't know or would prefer not to see. He doesn't show us to make us feel hopeless. He shows us so He can transform us to be like Him. I often go telling on someone in prayer only for God to show me how I am also a guilty party in the matter. He shows me my need to repent, and my need to see His perspective. Telling is as much about God correcting my offender as it is about God lovingly correcting me. So, when you go telling, be humble enough to receive the response. Yes, He comforts, but because we are His children, He also corrects.

So, the next time that husband, that coworker, that child, that friend now turned enemy pushes you, don't push back in your flesh; only complicating the matter. Run and tell your daddy on them in prayer and then sit still long enough to hear if you also need correction.

Scripture for Meditation:

Psalm 55:2 (NIV)

Cast your cares on the Lord and he will sustain you; he will never let the righteous be shaken.

Prayer Starter:

God, help me run and bring everything to you without reservation...

Reflection Questions:

Do you run and tell others about your problems or do you run to God?

Think about your present difficulties. Who have you told the most about it, your loved ones, or God?

Day 7: Is There Anything Too Hard for The Lord?

After many years of being barren, the Lord declares that Sarah within a year's time would have a son (Genesis 18:10-15). Sarah heard this, saw her circumstance and laughed silently to herself. She asked, "How could a worn out woman like me have a baby? And when my master-my husband is also so old?" (Genesis 18:12). Sarah laughed because she saw how impossible her situation was by man's standards. She heard the promise and immediately dismissed it because she thought of all the ways she couldn't bring it to pass. Considering her natural limitations, the promise of the Lord seemed like a big joke, unattainable. The Lord knowing all things, asked Abraham why Sarah laughed and then asks, "Is there anything too hard for the Lord?"

What impossible situation are you dealing with now? What promises has the Lord made to you that contradicts the barren areas of your life? Are you doubting and laughing at these promises because you have believed and accept what you see as your final story?

Time or any other limitations do not confine God. May I remind you as I remind myself that this is the same God who spoke "Let there be light," and there was, the God whose words have creative power. The God who parted the Red Sea and cause His people to walk across on dry ground. The same God who opened blind eyes, caused the lame to walk, and the blind to see. Yes, this is the God we serve. Sometimes when the impossibility is staring at us, it is easy to have amnesia and forget about God's resume. Let's continue to ask this question when tempted to laugh and doubt, "Is there anything too hard for the Lord?" In case you were wondering, the answer is a resounding NO! Stop laughing at what God has promised. Grab a hold by faith, declaring it with confidence, knowing there is nothing too hard for Him!

I Will Not Laugh

I look at my circumstances and take my eyes off you.

I become convinced that this is too hard for you to do.

But I get in the word and it reminds me of who you are.

It increases my faith and the chains of unbelief begin to fall.

I will not laugh; I choose to believe.

With you, there are no impossibilities.

Scripture for Meditation:

Jeremiah 32:17 (NLT)

O Sovereign LORD! You made the heavens and earth by your strong hand and powerful arm. Nothing is too hard for you!

Matthew 19:26 (NLT)

Jesus looked at them intently and said, "Humanly speaking, it is impossible. But with God everything is possible."

Prayer Starter:

God, your word says there is nothing too hard for you. Help me Lord not to just say it, but really believe it. Tear down the walls of doubt in my life...

Reflection Questions:

Are you doubting and laughing or are you believing God for your impossible situation?

Day 8: Press to Pray

I think about the woman with the issue of blood in Luke 8: 43-48. She bled constantly for 12 years and could find no cure. But when she pressed through the crowd and touched the hem of Jesus' robe, he healed her in an instant. The same is true for us when we press to meet Jesus in prayer. Prayer is a press, but it's necessary. It's my lifeline. I am amazed at what God does because of prayer. I can't allow life and the crowd to keep me from praying. I must press.

I Must Press

I show up to pray and you are already there.

You were there waiting for me.

I am in awe that when I press to get into your presence,

You meet me.

You tell me like you told her: *Your faith has made you well.*

But to touch you, to see you,

I must press through the crowd.

The crowd of my circumstances.

The crowd of my own thoughts.

The crowd of my pain.

The crowd of the internet.

Crowds can distract and discourage me and make me believe that the press is not worth it.

But I see my need for healing on so many levels.

I see that I will always NEED you.

I can spend my resources on things that guarantee that they will fix me.

But these temporal things can't stop the steady flow of my issues.

The pain doesn't go away.

But when I press, I touch you.

And in an instant, I am healed.

I feel the weight lift in your presence.

In your presence:

You affirm my faith.
You break curses.

Miracles happen.

I am transformed.

So, while the crowd will always be there,

I will continue to press to meet and touch you.

I WILL PRESS TO PRAY!

Scripture for Meditation:

Hebrews 11:6 (NIV)

And without faith it is impossible to please God,
because anyone who comes to Him must believes that
He exists and that He rewards those who earnestly
seek Him.

Prayer Starter:

Dear God, you see the things that threaten to keep me
from your presence. God, help me have a greater press
to get to you...

Reflection Questions:

What are the "crowds" in your life that keep you away
from Jesus?

Are you in the habit of pressing
through these crowds to get
to prayer, or do you allow
them to distract you?

Day 9: Addicted to Prayer

I must confess that I am addicted to prayer. Not because I am super spiritual, but because I am human with many frailties. I cannot function and my days seem to fall apart without prayer. I really am a hot mess without it--ask my husband and children. There is just something about throwing myself at the feet of Jesus and telling Him all my unedited thoughts. In prayer, I don't have to tell Him what I think He wants to hear. Instead, I tell Him exactly what I am feeling--the good, the bad and the ugly. Then I take Him up on His word and ask Him to fix me. Fix the chaos, the pain, and the hurt. I remind myself of Psalm 56:8 which states, "You keep track of all my sorrows. You have collected all my tears in your bottle."

Sometimes I can't find the words to pray and I sit and cry. I am fully convinced that He understands the meaning of each tear. While the cause of my pain may not immediately go away, just being in God's presence, crying like a baby, gives me peace beyond my understanding. I leave with confidence knowing it will be alright. I may not know how it will happen, but our time together reminds me it will all work out for my good.

Then there are those times I run to prayer begging the Lord to tell me I am not crazy for standing in faith even though I feel bullied by doubt and all his buddies. The times where the comments of others cause me to question if I am being too extreme, taking this faith thing a little too far. Ever been there? The times where I need to have the Lord comfort me and remind me that walking by faith will seem foolish to the world, but it pleases Him, and that's all that matters.

I also have times of carrying the burdens of those I love. I replay in my head how to fix them and their situation. The burden leaves me paralyzed because I want to make it all better. Then I am reminded I can pray and lay my burdens at his feet. I become even more confident when I remember that God hears my prayer and can change any situation, no matter how hopeless. So, I come to God on their behalf and do what I should have done in the first place...pray!

Then sometimes praise and adoration flow from my lips and I am overwhelmed with thanksgiving. The more I rehearse His goodness, the more I realize how awesome He is, and I don't want the moment to stop. I look for the pause button in these moments of sweet communion, hoping the phone won't ring and the children will remain asleep. Inevitably these moments of prayer must end, but the residue of praise remains.

Yes, I am addicted to prayer. I am not looking for a cure, just for more of His presence!

Scripture for Meditation:

1 Thessalonians 5:17 (NLT)

Never stop praying.

Colossians 4:2 (NLT)

Devote yourselves to prayer with an alert mind and a thankful heart.

Romans 12:12 (NLT)

Rejoice in our confident hope. Be patient in trouble, and keep on praying.

Prayer Starter:

Dear God, please help me to always make prayer my primary focus. There are many things that take my attention, but help me to prioritize prayer...

Reflection Questions:

Are you addicted to prayer?

If so, how has prayer benefited you? If not, how do you think you can benefit?

Day 10: A Great Distraction

Confession: I am easily distracted. I can begin the process of cleaning my living room and head to the kitchen to get something. Before you know it, my attention shifts to the kitchen and the living room is forgotten. I then get the bright idea to google great colors to paint my kitchen (the same kitchen that I know won't need painting for another year) and then drift off into researching colors for the closet. Sometimes the distractions are quite accidental, but most of the time I am actively looking for a distraction because I am trying to avoid doing what needs to be done or sometimes, I am just overwhelmed.

I remember not too long ago, I desperately needed to clean my house. However, I was *looking* for something to distract me. I didn't want to think or move. Then it happened. I heard the Holy Spirit whispering ever so gently, inviting me to allow Him to be my distraction. Now there is a thought for you! What if in my moments of wanting to be distracted, I run to the Lord. Isn't it interesting how we can accept that initial invitation to come to Christ for forgiveness of our sins and to find rest but fail to allow him to fully engage us after our initial acceptance? There is sometimes a disconnect, and we miss that coming to Jesus should be a daily habit, not a one-time event!

We look for distractions because we don't want to deal with whatever is before us. But we all know that after the distraction, the very thing we were trying to avoid is still there, waiting to be dealt with. However, when I allow the Lord to be my distraction, He gives me rest and I don't become overwhelmed or consumed by the thing I am running from. When I sit in His presence, I get refreshed, gain wisdom, find peace and abiding joy! It also redeems my time when I am in His presence. This prayer thing is very much a worthwhile distraction!

Scripture for Meditation:

Psalm 61:2-3 (NKJV)

From the end of the earth I will cry to you. When my heart is overwhelmed; lead me to the rock that is higher than I. For you have been a shelter for me, a strong tower from the enemy.

Prayer Starter:

Dear God, help me to grow in the habit of coming to you daily. Help me in becoming comfortable, bringing everything to you and not look for other things to distract me...

Reflection Questions:

Are there things you are trying to avoid?

Are you looking for things to distract you, or are you running to God in prayer to ask for help to complete what is necessary?

Day 11: Do Not Pray Like a Politician

Some politicians are notorious for telling voters what they want to hear. To win your vote, they make promises they know they won't keep. They sing us sweet lullabies of better days ahead. They go to great lengths and hire people to write speeches that will evoke loud applauses. Election time can become one big circus. If I am not careful, I can fall into the trap of praying like a politician.

God is not concerned about me giving speeches in prayer; telling Him what I think He wants to hear. He is not asking me to make empty promises. He is not asking me to have the well thought out phrases and giving Him my resume. None of that impresses Him.

Jesus prayed real RAW HONEST prayers, and He wants us to do the same. Jesus is inviting you and I to come and tell Him all, withholding nothing.

He invites me to cast all my cares on Him--telling Him the good, the bad and the ugly. Allow Him to see my heart, inviting me to replace my filth with His righteousness and giving me a greater level of freedom.

He invites me to come and tell Him RAW HONEST EMOTIONS...like when I really don't want to forgive because the offense seems too great and the offender never said sorry. He invites me to cry out and ask Him to help me go beyond my feelings and ask Him for the grace to walk in forgiveness as many times as I need to.

He invites me to be honest, take off my church face, abandon my well-crafted speeches and tell Him I feel doubt overtaking me. This doubt creeps in when I have been in the wilderness longer than I would like and I wonder if He has forgotten about what He has promised. He wants me to have raw conversations with Him about my doubts and then sit long enough to get His faith infused answer, giving me the proper perspective to continue to believe!

He invites me to be honest and tell Him that my flesh loves the applause of man making me sometimes more focused on pleasing them instead of pleasing Him. He wants me to be honest and tell Him I struggle to not think too much of myself. It is then He shows me how to be like Him, how to imitate His humility, something I cannot fabricate.

I officially resign from praying like a politician. I want to be a house of prayer, flowing in the power of God. Teach me Lord. How about you?

Scripture for Meditation:

Psalm 51:16-17 (NLT)

You do not desire a sacrifice, or I would offer one. You do not want a burnt offering. The sacrifice you desire is a broken spirit. You will not reject a broken and repentant heart, O God.

Prayer Starter:

God, help me put down all my guards in prayer and pray with sincerity...

Reflection Questions:

Are you comfortable being transparent with God in prayer, or are your prayers scripted and "safe"?

Why do you think it is difficult for you to pray honestly to God?

Day 12: No Pretending Honest Prayers

I used to be good at playing pretend, but then I got tired. Somewhere along the way, I realized that playing games can get old.

When I stopped pretending, that's when I learned how to pray.

Stop pretending that everything is ok when it is not.

Stop pretending like it doesn't hurt when it does.

Stop pretending I want to do the right thing when everything in me is screaming go left.

Stop pretending I am perfect, because I am not!

So, I pray.

Real prayer.

No script.

No pretense.

Honest, "*I don't want to do it God,*

This is just not fair God,

How come God?"

Child to parent dialogue.

My Good Father... He listens.

I cry.

I whisper the darkest secrets of my heart,

Thoughts I didn't even know were there, ugly thoughts.

Prayer is my therapy; I unload the burden.

He continues to listen.

Yes, I have a good father... I am blessed like that.

I am learning He is not looking for an act,

He requires honesty.

The honesty that scares nice church folks.

Yep, I know the right answer... I shouldn't think like that.

But what happens when I do,

And I must confess that sometimes I do.

I pray honest prayers.

No pretense 'cause that's outdated and ineffective.

In honest prayers, I am not the only one that speaks.

My good father He responds,

With love,

With His truth.

He knows that even in my brokenness,

Even in my humanity,

I have said yes to His will, yes to Him being Lord of my life.

A yes, I won't take back.

So, in my no pretending prayer,

He molds me,

He refreshes me,

He reminds me,

He corrects me,

He fills me again with His spirit,

Bringing an even greater death to me so I can live in Him.

Scripture for Meditation:

Psalm 139:23-24 (NLT)

Search me, O God, and know my heart; test me and know my anxious thoughts. Point out anything in me that offends you, and lead me along the path of everlasting life.

Prayer Starter:

God, help me understand that you are not looking for a performance when I come to pray, you are looking for honesty and humility. Help me, Lord, to be vulnerable in your presence...

Reflection Questions:

Is it hard for you to be honest with God in prayer?

Is it difficult for you to share the ugly parts of you with God?

Have you been praying no-pretending prayers?

Day 13: Prayer is the Ultimate Ice Breaker

I once attended a leadership conference, and the speaker used prayer as an icebreaker. He told us to find someone in the room we did not know and pray for her need. I quickly found a sweet young lady. We exchanged names, and she asked me with a smile, "How can I pray for you?" Before I could filter my thoughts and give her a general and "safe" prayer request, I was vulnerable and spilled personal information about myself. Information I would have preferred not to lead a conversation with, especially to a total stranger. But that was the point she wasn't a stranger she was my sister in Christ. There was a great sense of comfort as I shared. She listened with a smile, and then it was her turn. She gave her prayer request and then we took turns and prayed for each other. Then just like that, the ice broke for me. Whatever walls or inhibitions I had came down. God prepped my heart through prayer. This prayer set the stage for the rest of the conference; it was the icebreaker.

That simple demonstration impacted me. Allow me to explain. The speaker mentioned how we have complicated a simple thing. We go to extravagant lengths to do "church." But what if, what if we returned to one tradition mentioned in the bible... PRAYER! Prayer does not require special fundraising or man-made strategies. All it requires is a heart after God and a desire to see His kingdom manifested here on earth as it is in heaven. Real prayer that breaks the ice is not about proper grammar, volume, or even length, it is about the humility of heart and intimacy with God. I love to hear people pray who are connected to God. As they pour their hearts out to Him, I feel like I am getting the inside scoop between two friends. It's a beautiful thing to witness when the ice breaks.

However, life can beat us up and call us away from what matters the most which is a relationship with God. Sometimes we stay away from God for so long and He feels like a stranger to us. We wrestle with how to connect with Him, how to get over the awkwardness that is present. How do we break the ice on our heart? The answer is prayer. Just begin to speak to Him, He delights in hearing from His children. Have you ever had to have a difficult conversation with someone, and you are not sure where to begin? Prayer again is the answer. It helps to break the ice and set the atmosphere. I am not naïve to think everyone is receptive to prayer, however; it doesn't hurt to try. Prayer not only bridges the distance with God, but it also helps us in our relationship with others.

Scripture for Meditation:

James 4:8 (NIV)

Come near to God and he will come near to you. Wash your hands, you sinners, and purify your hearts, you double-minded.

Psalm 51:10 (NIV)

Create in me a pure heart, O God, and renew a steadfast spirit within me.

Prayer Starter:

Dear God, help me not to neglect communicating with you. You desire intimacy and not a distance between us...

Reflection Questions:

Have you ever felt distant from God?

Do you allow the distance to grow, or do you pray to bridge the distance?

Day 14: Confess, Forgive, and Move On!

We were having an ongoing problem in our home and my assumption was that the culprit was a particular child. For months as the problem continued, I would reprimand this child and he would vehemently deny it. I didn't believe him and the more he denied it the angrier I became. We recently had an impromptu devotion with the children because we all needed a spiritual tune-up. I shared Proverbs 28:13– "Whoever conceals their sins does not prosper, but the one who confesses and renounces them finds mercy." After reviewing this scripture with the children, I invited everyone to confess their sins to God. Right before bed, I was reminded of the reoccurring problem we had been having for months. I approached the one I assumed was the culprit and before I could finish my accusations, another child began to confess that he was the guilty party. All this time, he kept his sin hidden. It shocked me. I could see the shame on his face as he confessed, and I could tell he was expecting a negative response, but the grace of God overwhelmed me, and I responded accordingly. I told him that even though his actions were wrong, I was happy that he confessed his sins. I encouraged him to apologize to his brother-the one he allowed to carry the blame for all these months. What happened after that warmed my heart. The other brother who was accused all this time responded with grace. He let his brother know that he forgave him and just like that he carried on playing with his Lego. He didn't take the time to relish because he was finally vindicated. He forgave and moved on.

I had a few exchanges with them and went to my room and uttered a prayer of thanksgiving to the Father. I want my children to know Jesus, like for real know Him. I want them to respond to the convictions of the Holy Spirit. I want them to confess their sins. I want them to know the beauty of forsaking sin and receiving God's forgiveness. I want them to experience the grace that comes from true repentance. I also want them to freely forgive others and not hold on. The struggle with sin is real in our home, that I won't pretend! But this incident was a sweet reminder that God is at work, and He is greater!

I encourage you to, confess your sins when needed. Our sins not only impact us but it can impact others, so when necessary apologize to those who have been affected by your sin. If you are the one that has been offended, be merciful and receive the apology and move on, no need to remind the person of what they have done! In other words, respond with mercy- the way God responds to us when we repent.

Scripture for Meditation:

Psalm 28:13 (NIV)

Whoever conceals their sins does not prosper, but the one who confesses and renounces them finds mercy.

Prayer Starter:

God, help me to confess my sins to you and not try to hide them. Help me to also extend mercy to others when I have been offended...

Reflection Questions:

Are you in the habit of trying to hide your sins from God, or are you quick to confess them?

Are you currently holding on to any unconfessed sins?

Do you expect mercy from God but withhold mercy from others?

Day 15: Repentance is the Warm-Up

Most workout enthusiasts encourage you to warm up before exercising because it is crucial to an effective workout. It warms your muscles and increases blood flow to the heart while minimizing the risk of injury and increasing your energy.

The same is true for prayer. There are times we want to jump in COLD and our prayers feel like they are hitting the ceiling. We know we have done wrong but refuse to acknowledge it; we want to tell God all we need from Him. I have learned that REPENTANCE melts the frost off our hearts causing the grace of God to flow in our situation. It is arrogant to think we can just come into the presence of God expecting something without acknowledging our wrong. God is not pleased with arrogance. He makes it quite clear He resists the proud but gives grace to the humble (James 4:6). True repentance requires humility.

Sometimes we say sorry because we don't like the consequences of our actions but would return to that sinful action in a heartbeat if there were no consequences attached; if we knew no one would catch us. This is not true repentance. Repentance is saying, "God I am sorry, and I mean it. I regret what I have done, and I truly want to change. I want to turn from my sinful ways because I know it displeases you." Repentance says I want to turn my back on sin and run forward into the arms of Jesus. It is more than words; it is a shifting of the heart. It is an invitation to Jesus to come in and make right all that is wrong.

Yes, we prayed that initial prayer when we first came to Christ asking Him to forgive us of our sins; He did not intend for that to be our only prayer of repentance. As we go with Christ, His truth shines the light on the parts of us that need to change. We have to give up on trying to fix ourselves because the list is long. When we repent, we are inviting Jesus to shower us with HIS grace so we can walk in victory and for His strength to turn away from the thing that displeases Him. It is an ongoing process, but one that brings great FREEDOM!

Scripture for Meditation:

1 John 1:8-10 (NLT)

If we claim we have no sin, we are only fooling ourselves and not living in the truth. But if we confess our sins to him, he is faithful and just to forgive us our sins and to cleanse us from all wickedness. If we claim we have not sinned, we are calling God a liar and showing that his word has no place in our hearts.

Prayer Starter:

God, help me understand what true repentance means. I will not ignore my sins but confess them before you. I thank you for not condemning me but instead, you make your forgiveness available when I truly repent...

Reflection Questions:

Is there something you know you need to repent that may hinder your prayers? Anger? Jealousy? A bad attitude? I encourage you to pour your heart out to Jesus and receive his forgiveness so you can move forward in your prayers.

Day 16: Keep Coming

The Father invites us to come and pray about our past pain until He heals us. There is not a limit on our counseling sessions with Him. We know we are healed when we can see with clarity how God allowed that pain to work together for our good. One of the best "goods" that come from bringing our pain to God is the intimacy that is developed between us. I've seen God in a way I have never seen Him before because of deep wounds I kept bringing to Him.

The desperation that comes from desiring healing has a way of breaking down false pretense and formalities in prayers. I have experienced characteristics of God that were veiled because of legalism. When I am vulnerable with Him in prayer about my pain, I suddenly realize that He is not a distant God who is always looking for me to get it right. Instead, I come to know Him as a loving Father who wants to guide me with His truth. I no longer see Him as this God who is pointing His finger telling me to get over it and toughen up. Instead, I see Him as a compassionate and patient father who extends His grace and helps me to walk the path to maturity.

I also know that I have been healed when thanksgiving and praise flows from my lips instead of venom. The praise doesn't come from a place of naivety. Instead it comes from a deeper revelation of the goodness and sovereignty of God and His ability to redeem our pain when we come to Him. It is in the coming that we see how God used what the enemy intended to harm us with, as a launching pad for where He, wanted to take us. When we are healed, we look back on our painful experiences thanking God for His ability to bring beauty from pain.

Keep Coming

Keep coming to drink from the healing well.

Keep coming to drop the weight at His feet.

Keep coming,

Because it is in the coming

That healing happens.

Scripture for Meditation:

Isaiah 61:3 (NLT)

To all who mourn in Israel, he will give a crown of beauty for ashes, a joyous blessing instead of mourning, festive praise instead of despair. In their righteousness, they will be like great oaks that the LORD has planted for his own glory.

Romans 8:28 (NLT)

And we know that God causes everything to work together for the good for those who love God and are called according to his purpose for them.

Prayer Starter:

God, sometimes I get tired of bringing my pain to you. The process of healing seams so long, but hep me to keep coming to you...

Reflection Questions:

What pain are you currently experiencing?

Do you continue to bring your pain to God, or do you try to get healing on your own?

What does bringing your pain to God look like?

Day 17: The Healing Process Takes Time

Being healed from previous painful experiences is not automatic and is not always easy. We must make the choice to come to the mender of broken hearts and give him our hurt, continuously. It's a process. Don't become annoyed with the journey because you would prefer a microwave healing and remain at the surface. Resist the temptation to say one prayer, move on and pretend like it never happened. Denial is not synonymous with healing. Suppressed pain is a ticking time bomb, and it is just a matter of time until we explode! Go ahead, ugly cry in His presence, it's ok. Tell Him all of it--

Tell Him how much it hurt

Tell Him about your insecurities

Tell Him about your on and off desire to get revenge.

Confess the unwillingness to forgive and bitterness that may have festered in your heart.

Tell him about the pride that may be present that has driven you to prove them wrong.

Tell Him all...

AND

THEN

LISTEN

Listen as He tells you who He is because the pain made you doubt and accuse Him.

Listens as He tells you who you are because the pain made you forget.

Listen as He tells you how much He loves you

Listen as He tells you of the urgency of forgiveness.

Listen as He tells you that releasing the offense is not a nod of approval for what they did, but a healing balm for your soul.

Listen well and respond with obedience.

Scripture for Meditation:

Matthew 11:28 (NLT)

Then Jesus said, "Come to me, all of you who are weary and carry heavy burdens, and I will give you rest.

Psalm 147:3 (NIV)

He heals the brokenhearted and binds up their wounds.

Prayer Starter:

God help me acknowledge my pain in your presence and make room for you to bring healing. Help me to be patient and not abort the healing process...

Reflection Questions:

Are you in the habit of pretending like painful experiences never happened because it is too much work to face it?

Who do you tell the most about the pain in your past, humans or God?

Why do you think we are prone to vent to other flawed human beings instead of bringing our pain to a perfect God?

Day 18: I Am Ready to Let Go And Move On

There are parts of me that are fragile. Scarred from past hurts.

I love God.

I do.

But sometimes I don't look like He wants me to.

He has been showing me things about me.

Ugly things I have been carrying.

Things I need to let go of, to go to the next level. Things I didn't want to let go of... until now. Yes, I have prayed about it before, but I still held on because I felt justified.

But I recently cried and confiding in God, I told Him,

"I don't know how to let it go, but I want to. I really do. It is too heavy. I don't know how to let go of the pain, the offense, the hurt, the pride, false expectations, the jealousy."

But then He whispered,

"You don't have to let go in your own strength. Desire to purge these things, and your desire for purging invites me to deliver."
So I wept real hot tears. Tears of freedom.

I felt the weight lifting, and I am being transformed... again.

There is always another level to go to, but promotion always starts from the inside.

It is freeing to surrender these insecurities and scars to God.

No judgment, no condemnation from Him. Only pure love from my daddy when I tell Him.

I share my heart with you, not to glorify my weaknesses but to glorify a God who strengthens the weak. A God who understands the complexities of our past but challenges us to live beyond that, because the blood of His son made it right. Made me new. I am making the choice to let go of the past and move on and prayer is helping me to do just that.

Scripture for Meditation:

Isaiah 43:18-19 (NIV)

Forget the former things; do not dwell on the past.
See, I am doing a new thing! Now it springs up; do you
not perceive it? I am making a way in the wilderness
and streams in the wasteland.

Prayer Starter:

Dear God, I am tired of pulling this baggage around. I
am ready to release and move on. I forgive and make
the choice to move forward...

Reflection Questions:

Are you holding on to anything that is hindering your
ability to move forward; anger, offenses, unwillingness
to forgive others or even yourself?

Are you tired and ready to
move forward, or do you find
an odd sense of comfort in
holding on?

Day 19: Dear God Please Undo What I Have Done

She was not sleepy; I got her up 30 minutes prior. She was not hungry she gobbled down breakfast AND NO she was not wet. I changed her diaper right before she ate. But there was princess tugging at my leg demanding that I pick her up. Why? We spoiled her. All I could do was whisper in desperation, "Dear Lord please undo what we have done." Our 6th child, Faith, faced many complications before birth. We prayed for her healing and when God answered our prayers, the healing made us overjoyed. We brought our miracle home and spoiled her... real good. My husband and I were not the only culprits. Her siblings stayed in her face. If she cried, there were five other pair of hands ready to rescue her, it was a team effort. And we were dealing with the results. The prior scenario took place when my now 6-year-old was one. However, God used that day to bring something to my attention.

How many other times have I prayed that same prayer when I felt the consequences of MY poor choices.

I have yelled at my children in anger and unleashed misdirected frustration at them. I have felt ashamed when I see them deflate right before my eyes.

I have spoken negatively of others and I later hear my children with the same critical tone. I am forced to look in the mirror.

Sometimes I have had one too many "deserved" treats and I am left feeling sluggish, cranky and round.

All the above situations leave me asking the Lord to undo what I have done. I have learned that God won't go back in time and undo my mess. However, it is not all lost. When you have a surrendered heart, He provides the tools for you to move forward and the wisdom to make choices aligned with His will. My life testifies to the fact that repentance invites the Lord to masterfully redeem self-inflicted pain.

It is so easy to focus on all of our mistakes, all of our shortcomings, all the, "I knew better. why did I?" scenarios in our life. Perhaps you are dealing with the painful consequences of choices you made that were out of God's will. You have no sense of hope for the future, only regret for what's behind.

If you have not done so already, Jesus is lovingly inviting you to come to Him. Repentance is liberating and His forgiveness is the sweetest medicine I have tasted. While others may condemn and remind you of your mistakes, it's not so with my Jesus. Though we cannot go back in time and undo the mistakes, we can look to God for redemption and a better tomorrow.

Scripture for Meditation:

1 John 1:9 (NLT)

But if we confess our sins to him, he is faithful and just to forgive us our sins and to cleanse us from all wickedness.

2 Corinthians 5:17 (NLT)

This means that anyone who belongs to Christ has become a new person. The old life is gone; a new life has begun!

Prayer Starter:

God, I thank you for your ability to forgive and make all things new. I thank you that you will open my eyes to see the lessons I can learn from my past mistakes and move one...

Reflection Questions:

Have you made some poor choices lately and holding yourself captive to your mistakes?

Have you in humility brought those mistakes to God in prayer or do you feel you have to punish yourself?

Do you truly believe that God can redeem our past or do you feel hopeless and condemned?

Day 20: Avoiding God

Has life ever disappointed you, so you come up with the clever idea to avoid God? You find something to busy yourself with? Being busy is not a difficult thing for me, because there is always something to do. I have mastered the act of conveniently making myself busy when I don't want to deal with the issue at hand. Sometimes the issue is just too painful and requires too much self-inspection, so I avoid Him. It's not to say that I don't pray to God or acknowledge Him during these times. I do, but I remain on the surface. I make the choice to rush through my prayers and not quiet my spirit long enough to hear His response. I pray and "run" before God can address me. I can also sit still and yet allow my mind to be busy. I fill my thoughts with worry and manmade strategies to combat the disappointment at hand.

It is easy to justify thoughts and feelings when these thoughts are not being challenged. But to grow, I must allow God to challenge me. I should not avoid God especially in these moments of disappointment. The devil will deceive us to think God is the reason for the disappointment. This is deception at its finest and if we yield to it we miss out on connecting with the one who can comfort us during our time of disappointment and give us the proper perspective so we don't remain in that place!

As a parent, I want my children to run to me in their time of need instead of avoiding me. That is what good parents do. The counsel I give may not always be what they want to hear, but I always have their best interest in mind. It pains my heart when I know they are in a dilemma, but they refuse to come and talk to me. I want to help, and so it is with our heavenly father. He doesn't want us to avoid him. Life happens, disappointments take place. However, the more we avoid God, the bigger the problem gets! In moments of disappointment, run to Him in prayer instead of trying to avoid Him.

Scripture for Meditation:

Psalm 43:5 (NLT)

Why am I discouraged? Why is my heart so sad? I will put my hope in God! I will praise him again – my Savior and my God!

Prayer Starter:

God you alone are my refuge, help me to not run anywhere else in my moments of disappointment...

Reflection Questions:

Do you throw tantrums because of life's disappointments?

Do you find ways to conveniently avoid God because of these disappointments?

Is your anger towards the disappointments displaced, are you blaming God?

Day 21: Praying from a Humble Heart

In Luke 18:9-14 Jesus tells the story of two men who went to the temple to pray. One was a Pharisee and the other a dishonest tax collector. The Pharisee was so full of himself. He prayed the "perfect" prayer, telling God how wonderful he (the Pharisee) was. He pointed out how he was not like everyone else. He pats his own back through the entire prayer. He gave God his spiritual resume if you will. *"I don't sin, I don't cheat, I don't commit adultery, I fast not once but twice a week and to top it all off God, I tithe! Aren't I wonderful?"*

In contrast, the dishonest tax collector recognized his brokenness. He prayed from such a humble heart. He acknowledged that he was a sinner and begged God to have mercy on Him. He did not fill his prayers with platitudes. He prayed with humility. That pleased the Father.
If we are honest and honest is good; we can admit that we have been guilty of praying like the Pharisee.

Telling God how wonderful we are in prayer and reminding Him of all we have done can be an avoidance strategy. We somehow feel that focusing on our "spiritual" accomplishments, keep the spotlight off of all that we are not doing. We may give our money, but do we give the gift of forgiveness to the one that hurt us? We don't cheat on our taxes, but do we cheat God by not giving Him our time in prayer and the study of His word? Instead, we waste our time on social media and unfruitful activities. Checked boxes on our spiritual to-do list does not address the issues of our hearts.

It is also easy to compare ourselves to others in prayer. The question should never be, "how am I doing compared to others?" Instead, we should ask, "How am I doing compared to God's righteous standards?" An honest answer to this question sets the stage for a posture of humility in prayer. It reminds us of our DAILY need for God's mercy.

Scripture for Meditation:

Luke 14:11 (NIV)

For all those who exalt themselves will be humbled, and those who humble themselves will be exalted.

James 4:6 (NIV)

But he gives us more grace. That is why Scripture says: "God opposes the proud but shows favor to the humble."

James 4:10 (NIV)

Humble yourselves before the LORD, and he will lift you up.

Prayer Starter:

Dear God, help me maintain a posture of humility, acknowledging my need for you. I will not base my prayers on how well I think I am doing in comparison to others...

Reflection Questions:

Is it easy for you to admit your need for God in prayer?

Which one are you most like in prayer, the Pharisee or the tax collector?

Day 22: All is Well Because God is Good. Prayers of Thanksgiving

As of late, when asked how I am doing, my response is, "all is well because God is good!"

Yes, I agree, life can be tough, and problems are real.

Sickness happens.

Relationships fail.

Bills need to be paid.

Hearts get broken.

Rejection hurts.

BUT GOD IS STILL GOD, AND HE IS GOOD SO ALL IS WELL!

This statement is not a dismissal or denial of the difficulties that life brings. Instead, it is a choice to magnify God over my difficulties and to remind myself that all things will work together for my good. Why is it so easy for us to focus on the negative things around us while dismissing the overwhelming evidence of God's goodness constantly before us? On a morning not too long ago, I opened my bedroom blinds and was in awe of the beautiful sunrise that greeted me. I had to pause and take it all in. What I saw confirmed Psalm 19, "the heavens proclaim the glory of God. The skies display his craftsmanship." We have a choice. We can begin our day focusing on our problems and the business that awaits us, or we can acknowledge the goodness of God. You don't have to look very far to see it, creation testifies of His goodness. I see and acknowledge it so I will continue to say and live in the reality that, "all is well because God is good!"

I encourage you to pray prayers of thanksgiving each day. This practice helps you to focus on the goodness of God instead of your circumstance. Thank God for life. Thank him for his provision. Thank him for his protection. Thank him for his guidance. Thank him for being God! Get specific in your prayers of thanksgiving. For example, instead of saying, "God thank you for your provision," you can say, "God thank you that I have a roof over my head, clothes on my back and food to eat." Make thanksgiving a habit and you will also become convinced that all is well because God is good.

Scripture for Meditation:

Psalm 100:5 (NLT)

For the LORD is good and his love endures forever; his
faithfulness continues through all generations.

Prayer Starter:

God help me to be constantly aware of your
goodness...

Reflection Questions:

What declaration rooted in truth are you making
today?

What reasons do you have to be thankful?

List at least three of those
reasons below.

Day 23: Worrying is Overrated, Try Praying!

If I am not careful, I can think too much on a situation of concern. I have been guilty of overthinking things which leaves me spiritually and emotionally drained. Someone offends me and I play the offense over in my mind. I may say something to someone and later worry if I said too much. Did I say it in the wrong way? Has this ever happened to you?

Thinking too much opens the door to worry. If I am not careful, I can worry through the pain, instead of praying through it. Worrying allows your emotions to get the best of you. Living in your emotions can be deceptive. Trust me, I can tell you stories on this one. Worrying is an insult to God. It says, "I do not trust you. I do not believe you have my best interest at heart. You do not know what you are doing so let me worry my little finite heart out and come up with a solution." Worrying makes no sense!

The Lord invites us not to worry about ANYTHING but to pray about EVERYTHING!

Worrying is tragic while praying brings a peace that is out of this world. Prayer says, "Jesus not only do I want you to take the wheel, but I want you to pick up this vehicle and carry it." I cannot even sit in the passenger seat yelling out which way we should turn because I don't know. Prayer is a liberating experience.

Prayer:
-Lifts burdens that are too heavy to carry
-Brings order where there is confusion
-Gives hope for what seems hopeless
-Affirms me when human words have torn down

-Gives strength when my strength has failed
-Reminds me that nothing is too hard for God
-Gives me the self-control to close my mouth and allow God
to do the explaining.

Worry too much? I encourage you to change those thoughts
to prayer and get ready for God to overwhelm you with His
peace.

Scripture for Meditation:

Philippians 4:6-7 (NLT)

Don't worry about anything; instead, pray about everything. Tell God what you need and thank him for all he has done. Then you will experience God's peace, which exceeds anything we can understand. His peace will guard your hearts and minds as you live in Christ Jesus.

Prayer Starter:

Dear God, I trade in my worry for your peace. I make the choice to bring my burdens to you...

Reflection Questions:

What is your default response to problems, do you worry or pray?

Does worrying give you a false sense of control?

Day 24: Keep Calm and Pray On

In my first and only birthing class over 15 years ago, I learned that I should not let my emotions get the best of me when the pain from the contractions came during delivery. They recommended that I use a breathing pattern to help keep me calm through the contractions. I did not understand why there was such a strong emphasis on staying focused and breathing until that fateful December morning in the year 2003. I had NEVER felt pain like that before; it was unreal. The temptation was there to scream and totally lose it, but I REMEMBERED! I made up my own unorthodox breathing pattern when the excruciating pain from the contractions overwhelmed me. The breathing instead of screaming like a madwoman approach did not cause the pain to go away, but it helped to put me in a zone. I knew that there was no going back; I had to deliver the baby. The pain was a part of the package for life to come. Let me say that again, THE PAIN WAS A PART OF THE PACKAGE FOR LIFE TO COME. And so it is with life...

Many of my revelations come from my experiences as a wife and mother.

God reveals so much in what may appear to be mundane. But in my barefoot and pregnant, wiping noses, potty training, nursing, "I said no for the 10th time," "what do you want for dinner" seasons of life...I get a greater revelation of Jesus making the mundane magnificent! In life, Jesus is teaching me not to get distracted by pain. He is teaching me to keep calm and pray on.

The pain of waiting for an answer to prayer can cause you to lose it.

The pain of uncertainty and the realization that control is an illusion can cause you to lose it.

The pain from an alarming diagnosis from the doctor can cause you to lose it.

The pain from too little money and too many bills can cause you to lose it.

The pain from lost dreams and disappointments can cause you to lose it.

The pain of life is inevitable. If you are not careful, the pain can distract you. You can forget that you are in labor and though the pain is great, something beautiful awaits you on the other side. Do not get stuck in the middle of delivery and lose what God has promised. Screaming and letting your emotions get the best of you can prove detrimental. Today I encourage you to refocus, breathe in the goodness of God, and stand on His promises. Get in a zone and keep calm and pray on! Prayer births great things!

Scripture for Meditation:

Psalm 55:2 (NLT)

Give your burdens to the LORD, and he will take care of you. He will not permit the godly to slip and fall.

James 5:16 (NLT)

The earnest prayer of a righteous person has great power and produces wonderful results.

Prayer Starter:

God help me remember that panic does not fix problems, but prayer does...

Reflection Questions:

Are you often frazzled by life circumstances?

List uncertainties before you.

What has been your response - panic or prayer?

Day 25: Pray to Hear and Obey

Have you ever prayed to hear God's voice? Are you stuck, uncertain of your next moves and you need the Lord to speak to you? I have. I pour my heart out asking the Lord to provide clarity. However, when He gives me an answer I don't want, I go back with the same prayer request, "Oh God please let me hear your voice!" But what I am really saying is, "God I heard what you said, but I don't like that response. I don't want to do it! Can you please come up with another alternative?" He is God and I am not. It is pure arrogance when we as the created being scoff at what the creator tells us to do. For those of us who are parents, think about how silly it is when our young children think they know better than we do.

Even though I don't always like what I hear when God speaks it is always in my best interest to respond in obedience. Deuteronomy 28 lists all the blessings that follow when Israel obeyed God's instructions. We love to shout about those promises, 'blessed going out, blessed coming in!' But before you get to shouting, don't forget to read that passage in its entirety. The latter verses share the consequences of disobeying God. This passage reminds us that God communicates His expectations to His people. In return, He encourages His people to respond in obedience to those expectations. We are not to look for creative ways to alter what God expects of us.

God speaks to us in various ways. It may be in a dream, from His word, through other people, or just a strong inner knowing, among many other ways. Don't take for granted that the Creator of the Universe speaks to you! Even if it is not what you want to hear, take courage in knowing He won't lead you in the wrong direction. You cannot lose obeying God!

Do you find yourself with unfinished God tasks? You know, the things the Lord told you to do when you asked to hear His voice. The things you did not want to do. Yeah, those things. The start of a new day does not mean that God will change His mind. I encourage you to not only pray to hear God's voice. You should also pray for a heart to obey when He speaks even if it is not what YOU WANT TO DO. It requires humility to obey God, and that same humility unlocks His grace which enables us to follow through on His instructions.

Scripture for Meditation:

John 14:15 (NLT)

If you love me, obey my commandments.

Proverbs 3:5-6 (NLT)

Trust in the Lord with all your heart; do not depend on your own understanding. Seek his will in all you do, and he will show you which path to take.

Luke 11:28 (NIV)

He replied, "Blessed rather are those who hear the word of God and obey it."

Prayer Starter:

Dear God, please forgive me for my pride and disobedience. Help me sense the urgency in following your instructions. Even if it makes little sense or seem too difficult, God I receive your grace to obey the instructions you have given me in prayer...

Reflection Questions:

Are you constantly in the habit of disobeying God because you don't like the instructions, He has given you?

Are you praying for clarity you have already received?

Can you think of something you have prayed about, but you still haven't done it because it seems too difficult?

I encourage you to spend time in prayer to have the heart to hear and OBEY.

Day 26: Prayer Births Surrender

We should pray for God's will to be done in our lives. It sounds good on the surface, but the truth is sometimes God's will for our lives is hard. However, the more you pray, the more you can make the declaration in Matthew 6:10, "your will be done on earth as it is in heaven," because real prayer births real surrender. You do not get to this place overnight; it is a constant going back and asking God to work surrender in your heart. Surrender is not automatic, it is progressive, but we can hinder or halt the process altogether if we do not take time to pray. 2 Corinthians 12:8-10 details how Paul had a thorn in his flesh. Paul prayed three times asking God to remove this thorn. Constant prayer brought Paul to a place of surrender in accepting God's will for the thorn to remain. Paul was then able to gladly boast about his weakness so that the power of Christ could rest on him. In the natural it doesn't make sense, but only prayer can bring us to a place of rejoicing about our weakness.

Jesus, before He was crucified, was in agony in the Garden of Gethsemane. He went and prayed three times asking God if there was any way He could forgo the suffering. However, after constant prayer, Jesus came to the conclusion, not my will but your will be done.

Prayer Brings us to a place of saying to God:

- Your will be done when it hurts.

- Your will be done when it is uncomfortable.

- Your will be done when it means I will be persecuted.

- Your will be done when it means carrying my cross.You may be familiar with the acronym P.U.S.H. which is Pray Until Something Happens. However, that something shouldn't be focused on material things, but that something should be surrender. We often say pray until God gives us a yes, but we need to pray until we get to the place of giving God our yes. When we tell God yes, He then will give us a yes because our surrendered heart is in alignment with His will.

Scripture for Meditation:

Matthew 6:10 (NIV)

Your kingdom come, your will be done, on earth as it is in heaven.

Psalm 37:4 (NKJV)

Delight yourself also in the Lord, and he shall give you the desires of your heart.

Prayer Starter:

Dear God, help me to relinquish all control. Help me to have a surrendered heart that desires your will...

Reflection Questions:

Do you often go to prayer with a set agenda, or are you open to asking for God's will to be done in your life?

Do you only accept God's will when it is easy or are you totally surrendered?

Day 27: Is Suffering an Answer to My Prayers?

Many of us pray to be more like Jesus. We pray for God to perfect us. We pray to be patient. We pray to have hearts of humility and obedience. These types of prayers sound wonderful, but do we really understand the implications of what we are praying? Have we thought about the reality that it is trouble and not comfort that brings an answer to these requests?

Perfection and patience don't come from a steady stream of comfort but more from various trials we experience. Read James 1:2-5 for a good dose of this truth. And for obedience, the scriptures tell us in Hebrews 5:8 that "even though Jesus was God's Son, He learned obedience from the things he suffered." Yikes! You want to be humble you say? Philippians 2 tells us that Jesus was humble because He gave up His rights and left His place of comfort in heaven. He became a servant and took on a punishment He didn't deserve by dying on the cross for our sins. He didn't die a dignified death. Instead, He died a criminal's death on the cross.

Our culture has conditioned us to pursue comfort and avoid pain at all cost. However, prolonged comfort can stunt our growth. Think of athletes who want to excel in their sport and desire to emulate the great champions who came before them. These athletes do not spend all year pursuing comfort. Instead, they dedicate many hours throughout the year doing strenuous workouts to condition their body for success. Therefore, we should pray to be like Jesus, the greatest champion that ever lived.

As believers, this prayer is very much in order. However, be sure that when the trials come, you don't complain but rejoice, knowing your prayers are being answered! The trials come to build your faith and bring you to a place of looking like Jesus!

Allow me to get personal and share a journal entry I wrote in 2012 to further support this point.

At the beginning of 2011, the cry of my heart was for the more of God. I asked Him to fill me with His spirit in a way I had never experienced before. One year later I can reflect and say He did just that. He didn't quite answer my prayers in the way I had scripted it in my mind. Yeah, I got more of God, but it wasn't in a pretty package. I went through a "winter" season in my marriage, a month's stay in the hospital and 3 surgeries for my newborn baby, a long season of uncertainty, fatigue, helplessness, and TADA the result is the more of God. Yeah, not a pretty package but I received the desired result. My marriage is now even stronger, and God healed my baby; but even better, it was through my suffering I came to a "sweet" place in God. My suffering reminded me of my helplessness and the beauty of knowing Jesus! It was through my suffering I saw Jesus even the more. There is something about suffering that gives you the proper perspective if you surrender and rely on God's grace. I will be the first to confess that coming to that place of surrender and relying totally on God is a lot easier in theory than in practice. However, IT IS POSSIBLE!

Be encouraged, if you are in a season of suffering, try not to focus on how much it hurts. Pray and ask God to help you see how He is answering your prayers in the midst of suffering and the growth that is taking place. God often allows suffering to develop us, not to destroy us.

Scripture for Meditation:

James 1:2-4 (NLT)

Dear brothers and sisters, when troubles of any kind
come your way, consider it an opportunity for great
joy. For you know that when your faith is tested, your
endurance has a chance to grow. So let it grow, for
when your endurance is fully developed, you will be
perfect and complete, needing nothing.

Romans 8:17 (NLT)

And since we are his children, we are his heirs. In fact,
together with Christ we are heirs of God's glory. But if
we are to share his glory, we must also share his
suffering.

2 Corinthians 1:5 (NLT)

For the more we suffer for Christ, the more God will
shower us with his comfort through Christ.

Prayer Starter:

God, please help me see my
difficulties from your perspective.
Help me realize that as I yield
to you during my trouble, you
are perfecting me. In the end,
I will win because I will look
like you...

Reflection Questions:

Do you see your difficulties as a curse or as an opportunity to grow to become more like Jesus?

What opportunities are in your life now for growth?

Opportunities to be even closer to God and to look more like Him?

We don't always look at sufferings as opportunities for growth, but they are. Embrace your suffering, something beautiful awaits you on the other side.

Day 28: My Pain is Being Redeemed When I Intercede for Others

I once attended a corporate prayer meeting and witnessed something that brought me to tears. I heard the prayers of someone who had experienced deep pain intercede on behalf of another who was going through something similar. I cried because her past pain allowed her to intercede from a place of love. At that moment I realized that she had not wasted her pain, it was being redeemed.

Jesus is the greatest example of an intercessor. The pain He experienced on the cross was intercession for me and you. The stripes on His back, the crown of thorns on His head, the nail-pierced hands, the insults, the betrayal; none were in vain. His death purchased my redemption. My salvation proves He did not waste His pain. His intercession for me did not stop at the cross because Romans 8:34 tells me that He is now sitting at the right hand of the Father making intercession on my behalf.

When Adam and Eve ate of that fruit In Genesis 2, sin entered the world. As a result, we all have experienced the harsh realities of living in a fallen world. We all have stories of difficulties we have had to endure. What is yours? Is it rejection, betrayal, abuse? Those stories can either leave us bitter (wasting our pain) or push us to another level of intimacy with God and make us powerful intercessors (redeemed pain). When we are in Christ, we don't have to allow our pain to hold us captive. Christ has given us the victory over every painful situation we have or will ever endure. We can lament about our tragic stories or we can bring them to Jesus, allow Him to heal us and then raise us up to be powerful intercessors for those who are walking the same path of pain we once walked. The choice is yours, what will you do with your pain?

Scripture for Meditation:

Romans 8:31-35 (NIV)

What, then, shall we say in response to these things? If God is for us, who can be against us? He who did not spare his own Son, but gave him up for us all-how will he not also, along with him, graciously give us all things? Who will bring any charge against those whom God has chosen? It is God who justifies. Who then is the one who condemns? No one. Christ Jesus who died - more than that, who was raised to life – is at the right hand of God and is also interceding for us. Who shall separate us from the love of Christ? Shall trouble or hardship or persecution or famine or nakedness or danger or sword?

Prayer Starter:

Dear God, help me rise above my pain. I have endured some difficult things but help me see how you can redeem them through my willingness to intercede for others. Help me not to have an inward focus but see the needs of others around me and pray for them...

Reflection Questions:

What are you doing with the pain you have endured?

Are you wasting it or allowing the Lord to redeem it through your prayers of intercession for others who are going through something similar?

Day 29: Pray and Expect?

I pray and then what? Do I doubt, or do I wait in expectation for God to answer me, for Him to speak to my heart? Prayer is the easy part, but waiting with expectation, well that can prove to be a challenge.

I expect from those I trust. If I am worrying instead of expecting after I pray, then there is a trust issue going on and I have some backtracking to do in prayer. The first petition should then be to have the heart to obey God fully. How do I get to this place of trust and expectancy? It begins with a knowledge, appreciation and acceptance of the love God has for me. Romans 5:8 says, "But God showed his great love for us by sending Christ to die for us while we were still sinners." That's extreme love and anyone willing to die for a wretch like me is worthy of my love and my trust. It is easy to reduce the term "Jesus loves me" to just a simple song and not an extravagant life-changing truth. When I really get this, I can pray with boldness and wait with expectation for my loving trustworthy God to speak to my heart and show up.

We must also pray to stay in a place of expectancy no matter how long it takes for the answer to that prayer to manifest. It is easy to start off on day one with a great sense of expectancy but what is our response when the days turn to weeks; the weeks turn to months, and the months turn to years? The passing of time does not change God's mind and we should not allow it to change ours either. It is a fight to remain in that place of expectation, but continuous prayer makes it possible. Besides praying, you can also rehearse and thank God in advance for what you are waiting for. It is also encouraging to get in the word and read the stories of those who waited on God. Stories such as Joseph, and Abraham and Sarah in the book of Genesis. These will encourage and remind us of the faithfulness of God and remind us He is always working while we are waiting. Don't let the passing of time discourage you, continue to pray and expect from God. He is faithful!

Scripture for Meditation:

Psalm 5:3 (NLT)

Listen to my voice in the morning, Lord. Each morning I bring my requests to you and wait expectantly.

Romans 5:8 (NLT)

But God showed his great love for us by sending Christ to die for us while we were still sinners.

Prayer Starter:

God, help my trust in you to grow. Show me how to pray with a confident expectation knowing you are trustworthy and that you hear me. You know of the disappointments from my past that cause me to doubt when I pray. Fill my heart with faith...

Reflection Questions:

Do you pray and wait with expectancy that the Lord will speak to your heart and answer? Or do you often doubt He will answer?

Why do you doubt God? Is it due to past disappointments, or a lack of revelation of how much He loves you, etc.?

Day 30: Pause to Pray and Then Proceed

I was diagnosed with alopecia and my hair loss had taken a turn for the worse and I needed something—fast. The beautician told me it was medical glue and the hairpiece would look natural. The price was ridiculous, but she rambled off a list of names of celebrities whose stylists used said "medical" glue to get them picture ready. I was desperate and gullible—a bad combination. After the consultation, I went home and ~~asked~~ begged my husband to let me get it--On credit that was, because we did not have that amount of cash lying around. Not once did I consider praying about it. As far as I was concerned, this was a godsend.

Seeing my panic and desperation, my husband agreed to let me put this SUPER EXPENSIVE hairpiece on credit. Within a few weeks, the medical glue began to produce non medical results. I broke out with sores on my scalp because of an allergic reaction to the glue and had to have the hairpiece removed. The beautician offered no refund, and I was left with a head full of sores. That was a very expensive lesson on the detriment of not pausing to pray before proceeding!

Admittedly, I have jumped headfirst into many decisions that seemed like a good idea. I am learning and, by the grace of God, I don't want to continue to make the same mistakes. I find it dizzying going around the same mountain. Recently, another test came. I learned of an opportunity to grow in my gift as a writer. The program is legitimate. I read article after article and watched many videos of testimonials on the success of the program. I wanted in! The class had a large price tag attached to it, and rightfully so, it is an EXCELLENT class. We are actively trying to get out of debt and be good stewards of our finances, so putting this class on a credit card was not an option.

I mentioned the opportunity to my husband and, this time around, we paused and prayed before proceeding. I inquired via email about scholarships and different payment plans; all requests were denied. On one hand, I was disappointed because I really wanted to take the class. On the other, I was also encouraged (I participated in the teacher's free webinar which was excellent) because I knew that I had made the right decision and passed the test.

This principle of pausing to pray before we proceed with making decisions is echoed in Proverbs 3:5-6. This passage tells us that we are to trust in the Lord with all our heart, and not to lean on our own understanding. We are to acknowledge God in all that we do and allow Him to direct our path. Too many times we don't stop to consult God before making decisions and inevitably we end up bumping our heads. No matter how good the opportunity may look, I encourage you to pause to pray. Allow the Lord to direct your path, and once He responds, then you can proceed in faith!

Scripture for Meditation:

Proverbs 3:5-6 (NKJV)

Trust in the Lord with all your heart, and do not lean on your own understanding. In all your ways acknowledge him, and he will make straight your paths.

Prayer Starter:

Dear God, help me to take the time to pray before I make decisions...

Reflection Questions:

What major decisions are before you?

Are you quick to make decisions without first consulting the Lord?

Day 31: What Do You Do When You Don't Know What to Do?

What do you do when you don't know what to do and you are trying to make sense of it all?

What do you do when you find out what to do, but you don't want to do it because it is hard?
What do you do when you are holding the pieces of the puzzle in your hands and you are not sure where they fit?
What do you do when you have entered a new season and you are struggling to find your rhythm?
What do you do when you have so many good ideas swirling in your mind and you become overwhelmed because you don't know which one to pursue in this season?
What do you when you hurt because you know change is necessary, but you are afraid of the unknown?
What do you do when you are convinced you heard the Lord but then realized you didn't?
What do you do when emotions come to the surface you didn't know were there and you are not sure how to deal with them?
What do you do when your inadequacies stare you in the face and you don't know how to respond?

WHAT. DO. YOU. DO?

You pray.

And I did!

I am glad it's possible.

Possible for me to boldly take my "I don't know what to do self" to the throne of grace to find mercy and grace in my time of need.

Problems don't immediately disappear and not all my questions get answered but it renews my mind and restores my peace.

And I am reminded, that even if I don't know, He does.

So I rest In Him.

I trust Him.

I surrender with reckless abandonment to the one who knows exactly what to do when I don't!

Scripture for Meditation:

Psalm 18:2 (NLT)

The LORD is my rock, my fortress, and my savior; my God is my rock, in whom I find protection. He is my shield, the power that saves me, and my place of safety.

Psalm 43:5 (NLT)

Why am I discouraged? Why is my heart so sad? I will put my hope in God! I will praise him again – my Savior and my God!

Prayer Starter:

Dear God, help me remember that you are not expecting me to have all the answers. Instead, you want me to come and seek your face for guidance...

Reflection Questions:

What is your response when you don't know what to do? Do you try to figure it out on your own or do you run to God in prayer?

Day 32: What Should I Do While Waiting on God to Answer My Prayers?

I have fallen prey to the microwave mentality. I have made the mistake of approaching prayer the same way. I want God to answer the prayer as soon as I say 'amen'! That waiting thing, well that is just so biblical. I think about Hannah in 1 Samuel and the many times she prayed and begged God for a baby. Each time she came away with her prayers unanswered. I also think about Elizabeth and Zachariah. In Luke 1, it tells us they were faithful and upright before God yet, for years God told them no to their desire for a baby.

What did they do after they received a 'no' from God? Did they walk away from Him? Absolutely not! Hannah didn't stop going to the temple to offer sacrifices to God because she didn't get what she wanted. Zachariah didn't hang up his priestly robe and forsake his duties because he didn't get what he wanted. They continued to worship, even in their pain they worshipped, even in the denial they worshipped, even in the shame attached to bareness they worshipped. And guess what, it was in that place of continuous worship that God met them and gave them each a yes!

Hannah got her yes when she was in the temple. I love the rawness of this story. I love that Hannah didn't pretend in her prayers. I love that even in her distress, she still came to worship, she brought it all to God! It broke her, but she still came to worship. And it was in that place of worship that God met her and gave her a yes.

The same is true of Zachariah, it was in that place of worship that the angel came to announce the birth of his soon to be son, John The Baptist. The scripture says he was in the temple offering incense of prayers to the Lord. I don't think Zachariah was expecting anything from God since both he and his wife were old. But the 'no' he received from God did not keep Zachariah from worship. He still came to perform his priestly duty, and it was at that place of offering burnt incense to the Lord that God sent the angel Gabriel to answer His prayer; because perhaps he had stopped praying. God still gave Him a yes!

It is so easy for us to let the wait pull us away from God, instead of letting it push us closer to Him. So back to the original question, what do I do while waiting on God to answer my prayer... I worship! Even if I am broken, I worship, even if I feel like I am at my wits' end and can't hold on anymore, I worship, even if it has been years and everyone seems to pass me up, I worship. It is in my place of worship that God meets me!

I woke up on my 41st birthday and one of the first things I did was rub my hand on my head looking for the sign He had finally answered this long-standing prayer request. I told Him that this would be the best birthday gift. I thought He told me He would do it, that this was finally my time. I was wrong. Sadly, the familiar bald spots created by alopecia and scattered hair met the touch of my hand. I felt the disappointment trying to overtake me, but I fought against it. I thought on the goodness of God, and where He has brought me.

No, I'm not a millionaire, but at 41 years of age, I am a rich and fulfilled woman.

I am living on purpose! I am at peace. I have true joy. I am blessed beyond measure.

And I know God in an even more intimate way.
So I got up looked at my mostly bald head reflection in the
mirror and sang a song of rebellion against disappointment!
Restoration of my hair will come; of that I am certain. In the
meantime, this song will become my anthem because I will
worship as I wait.

I WILL WORSHIP SONG

What will I do As I wait on you?
I will worship
I will worship
Time does not change your mind
You are not a man that you should lie
So I will worship
I will worship
The doubts are trying to silence me
Lord help my areas of unbelief
By faith I declare
I will see what you have promised
Because you are God!
You are faithful!
I can trust you
So I will worship
I will worship

Scripture for Meditation:

Isaiah 40:31 (NLT)

But those who trust in the LORD will find new
strength. They will soar high on wings like eagles.
They will run and not grow weary. They will walk and
not faint.

Psalm 27:13-14 (NIV)

I remain confident of this: I will see the goodness of
the Lord in the land of the living. Wait for the Lord; be
strong and take heart and wait for the Lord.

Prayer Starter:

Dear God, the wait can be so overwhelming, and it is
so easy for me to lose hope. Help me, Father, to come
to the place of worship as I am waiting. Father help me
not to let the wait distract me and drift further from
you. Lord, let the wait bring me closer to you...

Reflection Questions:

What prayer are you waiting for God to answer?

What have been your responses while waiting? - complaints or worship?

Day 33: The No Was for My Good

It was painful. I cried. I was angry. I questioned God. In my finite mind, I felt that I knew best, and that best should have been a yes to my prayers. Time has passed and I now have the right perspective. I now can see that the no was for my good.

Isn't it funny how we think we know better than God and then have enough nerve to get an attitude when He doesn't answer our prayers the way we as the created being thought He should?

There are many reasons God gives us a no in prayer. I would like to discuss two of those reasons. The first glaring reason is that the thing we are asking for is not His will for our lives. He knows that a yes to that petition would make us drift from Him. He is a loving God, so He is more concerned about the state of our soul than He is about our temporary happiness. Sure, the no disappointed you, go and ahead and get all the cries of disappointment out. However, after the tears stop flowing and you have a moment of mental and spiritual clarity, you will thank Him because He knows what is best for you.

The next reason is that the thing we are praying for is God's will for our lives, but this is not the season for us to have it. A gift given prematurely can prove to be a burden. If I am not at the place to receive what God has for me, I will not have the bandwidth to steward it. That which should have been a blessing then turns out to be a curse. Calm down, take the no... it's temporary. Trust God's timing. The best illustration I can think of to show this point is that of a teenager who has a large sum of money that is due to him when he becomes a trusted adult. He can come at 16 to cash in on what is his, but his parent would do well to tell him no because at 16 he does not have the same ability to steward those finances the same way he would at 26 years old. God gives us a no because he knows that we have maturing to do.

Both instances described above shows that God's 'no' is an act of love and not one of cruelty. Say it with me, "That 'no' was for my good!" Rest knowing God knows best.

Scripture for Meditation:

Jeremiah 17:7-8 (NIV)

But blessed is the one who trusts in the Lord, whose confidence is in him. They will be like a tree planted by the water that sends out its roots by the stream. It does not fear when heat comes; its leaves are always green. It has no worries in a year of drought and never fails to bear fruit.

Prayer Starter:

God, take away all bitterness I may have in my heart for all the times you told me no. Help me Lord not to be prideful and think I know better than you. Help me rejoice in knowing that your no was for my good...

Reflection Questions:

List at least two times God said no to your prayers.

How did you respond?

Did you have the proper perspective?

Are you still looking for ways to make those prayers come to pass in your own strength?

Day 34: After I Get My Yes

What you do after God has answered your prayers reveal your motives. Do you take your yes from God and try to live your life without Him, or do you take your yes and allow it to draw you closer to Him? Many times, we pray and are more obsessed with getting the answer we want instead of wanting the one who answers prayers.

Have you ever been in a bad place and promised God that you will surrender all and serve Him if He answers your prayers? When we don't make good on these promises we waste the good that could have come from that place of suffering, we miss out on a closer relationship with God. I have observed people cling to God in a difficult season of their life. I see them attend services, get in their word, fast and pray. However, once there is a breakthrough and prayers get answered, their commitment feigns. The question then is, was I pursuing God for His stuff instead of His heart. This approach reduces God to a genie who we want to grant our every request instead of a loving Father who desires intimacy with His children.

Think about it, we can get all the "yes' "for the temporary things we desire, but what will it mean if we don't have God? Am I saying it is wrong to pray for temporal things such as a spouse, money to pay your bills, or good health? No, absolutely not! There are many scriptures that encourage us to bring our desires to God in prayer. What I am saying is that a closer relationship with God should always be our end goal. What a tragedy to get all we desire and miss out on the greater, which is intimacy with God.

After I Get My Yes

The temporal fades and cannot bring lasting joy.

So, while I will rejoice in my yes, help me to keep a steady gaze on you.

After I get my yes,

I will continue to worship.

I will continue to show up to commune with you.

I will give my yes to you!

Scripture for Meditation:

John 4:23 (NLT)

But the time is coming – indeed its here now – when true worshipers will worship the Father in spirit and in truth. The Father is looking for those who will worship him that way.

Prayer Starter:

Father help me not to pursue you ONLY because I want something from your hand. Help me to desire a relationship with you above all else...

Reflection Questions:

Take times to reflect. Are you more concerned about getting your yes to prayer than you are about getting closer to God?

Day 35: Don't Answer Your Own Prayers

We pray. Then we wait. And wait. And wait. We become impatient. We come up with the clever idea that God needs our help, so we create a plan to answer our own prayers! Then we create an even bigger mess in our life. Ever been there? Confession: I have, more times than I would like to admit. Thankfully, I am becoming a little wiser and learning that waiting on God is worth it. God is not running out of ways or time to answer the prayers we pray. He is not looking for us to concoct dead-end answers to our own prayers.

Sarah had to deal with this harsh reality in the book of Genesis. God promised her husband Abraham that they would have a son. Ten years passed and nothing happened. It appeared as if time was working against them, neither of them was getting any younger. To "help" God out, she came up with the clever idea to answer her own prayers for a child by telling her husband in Genesis 16 to sleep with her maidservant, Hagar. The custom of the day was that if your maid had a baby, you can consider the baby as your own. It seemed like a good plan, but it backfired. The events that took place after the child Ishmael was born is reminiscent of a soap opera. It was baby mama drama for real. To put it mildly, it was a hot mess. Sarah ended up putting out Hagar and Ishmael after it was all said and done. Isn't it interesting how we can end up despising the thing we thought would be an answer to our prayer?

When we look for ways to answer our own prayers, it shows that prayer is just a formality for us, a means of just going through the motion. We pray because we know that's what we should do not because it is what we want to do. News flash: God sees the discrepancies in our heart with this approach. Yes, there will be times when we pray and God gives us directives on what to do for Him to answer the prayers. That differs from just coming up with the ideas on our own on how to answer the prayer.

In the wait, He is teaching us valuable lessons. Don't rush or complicate the process, wait on God!

Scripture for Meditation:

Psalm 46:10 (NLT)

Be still and know that I am God!

Prayer Starter:

Dear God, please help me wait on you and not run ahead of you trying to answer my own prayers. Help me trust that your timing is perfect...

Reflection Questions:

Are you still waiting on God to answer your prayers?

What are some things you have done to help you as you wait?

Day 36: Holy Ghost Wildfire

I have really been thinking about the fire of God lately and frankly I DON'T WANT TO SHAKE IT. I don't want it to be a fleeting thought.

The more I go with God, the more I hunger for His fire--The fire that purges. I want to look more like Him... not thinking of myself more highly than I ought to, not striving to please man, not having an inward focus, and not putting limits on my ability to love. I want His supernatural love to flow through me, an overflow! This can't happen without the fire purging me. In Isaiah 6:5, the prophet Isaiah was undone when the glory of the Lord entered the temple. Isaiah was suddenly gravely aware of who he was when compared to a holy God and he exclaimed, "My destruction is sealed, for I am a sinful man and a member of a sinful race." In response to Isaiah, the angel took a coal from the altar of the Lord and placed it on Isaiah's lips, and told him, "see this coal has touched your lips. Now your guilt is removed, and your sins are forgiven," (Isaiah 6:6). That fire, that purging, created a deeper yes in Isaiah's spirit that when the Lord asked, "Whom should I send as a messenger to my people? Who will go for us?" Isaiah respond, "Lord, I'll go! Send me."

I also want the boldness that the fire brings so I can testify without hesitation to a dying world that Jesus is Lord. I want to operate in boldness and not allow the possibility of being persecuted and not being liked paralyze me. I want to speak His unpopular truths without reservation even though I know there will be a direct backlash. I want to say like Paul said in Romans 1:16, "I am not ashamed of the gospel of

Christ because it is the power of God unto salvation to everyone that believes."

I can't get to this place without His fire. I can't live beyond what is normal without His fire. I won't be willing to push past people pleasing and color outside the lines without His fire. Yes, God I want a Holy Ghost wildfire in me. I want you to set a fire down in my soul! I still believe He makes visitations like He did on the day of Pentecost in Acts Chapter 2.

I can't start this fire on my own, nor can I sustain it without seeking His face. Prayer starts and maintains the fire I long for. Without prayer, the fire fades. Prayer stokes this fire!

Scripture for Meditation:

Jeremiah 20:9 (NIV)

But if I say, "I will not mention his word or speak anymore in his name," his word is in my heart like a fire, a fire shut up in my bones. I am weary of holding it in; indeed, I cannot.

Luke 24:32 (NIV)

They asked each other, "Were not our hearts burning within us while he talked with us on the road and opened the Scriptures to us?

Prayer Starter:

Father help me hunger for your presence, for your fire. Help me understand that without a connection to you, there will be no fire at all. Help me be mindful of the distractions in my life that will keep me from coming to you in prayer to keep that fire going...

Reflection Questions:

Have you been crying out for the fire of God ton consume you so you can look more like Him?

Have you been spending time in prayer to stoke that fire?

Day 37: I Received More Than I Asked For

I'm learning more about God. There are so many facets of His character I didn't understand, but the more I learn the more I want to know. I desire to go deeper in Him! I'm experiencing the tenderness of His heart, and I'm blown away because I didn't know. I understand more. I see and feel it. This knowledge and first-hand experience compel me to weep and worship.
True worship.

No keyboard in the background. No praise and worship team encouraging me to lift my hands. Just a me and God kind of worship. I sing songs that have never been sung, they flow from the deepest parts of my heart and they reflect my gratitude. Worship where I can "feel" His presence and I am undone!

I used to mourn over my problems and unanswered prayers; not anymore, because they are the tools that God used to give me a greater revelation! Desperation to have my problems solved and prayers answered brought me to a place of consistent prayer. I was faithful to show up and beg God to move on my behalf. But somewhere along the way, something shifted. I long to talk to Him and it is not always about my problems or what I want; sometimes I just want to pour out my adoration because I now know Him in a greater way. I am certain the answer to my prayers will come, and the promises will be fulfilled-and frankly, I want them to. But I am content because I have attained even more. I now have greater intimacy with the one who has loved me with an everlasting love! I have indeed received more than I initially asked for.

I Received More Than I Asked For

I came for my prayers to be answered

But I received more.

Jesus you are the more,

More than enough.

Scripture for Meditation:

Psalm 27:4 (NIV)

One thing I ask from the LORD, this only do I seek:
that I may dwell in the house of the Lord all the days
of my life, to gaze on the beauty of the LROD and to
seek him in his temple.

Prayer Starter:

Dear God, please help me to not just focus on my
prayers being answered. Help me to desire more of
you...

Reflection Questions:

What is your main motive when you go to pray, is it to
get all your prayers answered or to get more of God?

Day 38: Prayer Journaling. Pay Attention God Is Answering

I have a prayer journal. In it, I record praise worthy moments, prayer requests, answers to prayers, and any insights the Lord gives me during my prayer and bible study time. When writing in my journal, I don't focus on proper grammar and format. As I put ink to paper my unedited thoughts flow. I am writing for an audience of two, me and God. This approach allows me to write without inhibition, the experience is liberating. Sometimes as I write, thoughts and feelings come to the surface I didn't realize were there. Also, when I journal in the morning without distraction, I am amazed at how much God reveals. This has taught me that when I position myself to spend time with God, He shows up and gives revelation!

In moments of discouragement, I have been able to go back and read different promises God spoke to my heart that I wrote and the prayer request He has answered. These recorded thoughts, revelations and prayers answered helps to give me focus and direction for the future. We must not limit God's ability to speak to us when we are writing. If you don't consider yourself a great writer, there is no need to worry. Remember, you are writing for edification and not a grade. There are many instances in scripture that God instructs an individual to write what they saw or what He revealed to them. Daniel, Joshua, and John in the book of Revelation are a few examples.

I try to go back and write the date or how God answered a specific prayer request. There is something about being deliberate with recording prayer requests and the answers that come. It makes me more aware of how God is responding. So often I pray, God answers, and for various reasons, I miss it. Sometimes it's because I was not praying in faith and I didn't expect God to move. Or I prayed and God answered but not in the way I wanted and expected him to. My prayer journal helps me to be more sensitive, more alert to the ways God is moving. Every day I have something praiseworthy to record. EVERY DAY! It's amazing. And as I go back and read the answers to prayers, it builds my faith and encourages me to keep on praying.

Scripture for Meditation:

Jeremiah 30:2 (NIV)

This is what the LORD, the God of Israel, says: "Write in a book all the words I have spoken to you."

Prayer Starter:

Dear God, help me be diligent in recording the ways I have seen you move on my behalf, so I may use it as a source of encouragement in future days. Help me be aware of how you are answering my prayers...

Reflection Questions:

Can you list at least three prayers God has recently answered?

Are you often aware of the answers or do you forget what you prayed?

Day 39: Writing Your Prayers. A Prayer for Putting on The Whole Armor Of God

At times, I sit and write my prayers. This approach does not make my prayer ineffective. Below is an example of a prayer I wrote based on Ephesians 6:10-18 that speaks of putting on the armor of God. Just in case you didn't know, I am here to inform you we are in a war. We are not fighting against flesh and blood, so we cannot use carnal weapons to fight.

Dear God, thank you for showing me you are not calling me to be strong in my power but to be strong in your mighty power. Help me recognize that my strength fails, and my power is limited but you are all-powerful. Teach me, Lord, to stand in your power that is MIGHTY! Father, I see how you used those that stood in your power in mighty ways. You used the apostle Paul to preach your gospel with great conviction, rebuke the hypocrites and heal the sick. He did so without reservation or fear of losing his life. You used the prophet Elijah to call down fire from heaven and stand against the prophets of baal. You gave them the power to stand and to obey.

Help me Lord to put on all of your armor so I can stand firm against all strategies and tricks of the devil. Help me to not forget that the enemy is after me. He came to kill, steal and destroy. He has laid traps for me, but I thank you God that your armor is enemy proof. I thank you that I don't have to be afraid of the tricks of the enemy. No weapon formed against my mind, my body, my children, my marriage, my purpose NO NOT ONE WILL PROSPER!

Father help me recognize who the real enemy is. Help me be mindful that I am in a war but not with a natural enemy. I will not get distracted by becoming upset with people and miss the spirit that is operating behind them. I will remember that I am not wrestling against flesh and blood but against the evil rulers of the unseen world, against those mighty powers of darkness who rule this world, and against wicked spirits in high places, in the heavenly realm.

Lord, you tell me to use every piece of your armor so I can resist the enemy in the time of battle and when the battle is over, I will still stand firm. I declare that because of your shed blood and your victory over death I have already won every battle! EVERY SINGLE ONE! I will not be fearful. God let a spirit of boldness overwhelm me knowing that even after the battle is over, I will still stand, not wobbling but standing firm!

Make me a bona fide warrior, one that puts on the belt of truth and the breastplate of righteousness. My righteousness is as filthy rags, but I thank you God that I can now take on the righteousness of God. You have clothed me with righteousness. I thank you God that for shoes I will put on the peace that comes from the good news, the good news that I will not be ashamed of. The good news that is the power of God that brings salvation to everyone that believes. I thank you God that I have faith as my shield to stop the fiery arrows aimed at me by the enemy. God, I won't buckle under pressure. I will not doubt you. I will not walk by sight. I will stand in faith knowing that without it I cannot please you. Knowing that whatever is not of faith is sin! It pleased you that Abraham had faith, and God I am a spiritual descendant of Abraham, so I take on the shield of faith!

I will put on salvation as my helmet. The salvation that gives me the mind of Christ. I thank you that I have the sword of the Spirit which is the word of God. The living and powerful

word of God, the word that cuts straight to the core. The word that is powerful and active and sharper than any two-edged sword. Thank you, that I will imitate Jesus and use the word to combat the devil when I am in a wilderness season. I will not yield to the voice of the enemy when I am most vulnerable, depleted, hurt and when the pain is overwhelming. I will use the sword of your word to fight. When the enemy comes to whisper that I am worthless and that I am without purpose I will use the sword of your word to rebuke the devil declaring that you knew me before you formed me in my mother's womb. You have great plans for me, plans to give me a future and a great end. I will not wallow in self-pity when everything seems to work against me. I will declare that all things are working together for my good because I love you and I will press toward the purpose you have for me. When the devil tries to make me feel condemned for past mistakes, I will fight with the word declaring that I am not condemned. I am forgiven. I am new. When he attempts to attack my body with sickness, I will declare with a boldness that by your stripes I am healed! Each day, I will put on the armor of God!
IN JESUS' NAME I PRAY AMEN!

Scripture for Meditation:

Ephesians 6:10-18 (NIV)

Finally, be strong in the LORD and in his mighty power. Put on the full armor of God, so that you can take your stand against the devil's schemes. For our struggle is not against flesh and blood, but against the rulers, against the authorities, against the powers of this dark world and against the spiritual forces of evil in the heavenly realms. Therefore put on the full armor of God, so that when the day of evil comes, you may be able to stand your ground, and after you have done everything, to stand. Stand firm then, with the belt of truth buckled around your waist, with the breastplate of righteousness in place, and with your feet fitted with the readiness that comes from the gospel of peace. In addition to all this, take up the shield of faith, with which you can extinguish all the flaming arrows of the evil one. Take the helmet of salvation and the sword of the Spirit, which is the word of God. And pray in the Spirit on all occasions with all kinds of prayer and requests. With this in mind, be alert and always keep on praying for all the LORD's people.

Prayer Starter:

Dear God, help me to daily put on the armor of God...

Reflection Questions:

Do you find you often fight your battles using carnal weapons?

Have you forgotten that it is a spiritual battle you are fighting?

Day 40: 5 Tips to Help You Become More Comfortable Praying in Front of Others

Corporate prayer is a beautiful thing and I enjoy hearing others pray. However, for some, praying out loud in a group setting can be terrifying. Below are things to consider when praying out loud that will help to ease anxiousness.

1. Spend time in personal prayer. Praying to God in private makes it easier to pray to Him in public. Pour your heart out to Him. Learn to become comfortable in His presence and give Him a chance to speak back to you. This time will help to develop intimacy with God and hopefully help you become more comfortable praying in front of others.

2. Study God's word so you can know His will, this will improve your prayer life. 1 John 5:15 tells me that God hears me when I pray His will and I can be confident He will grant my request. Studying His word assures me I am praying His will, because His will is in His word. When you pray in front of others, you will then have something to say because you have been in your word.

3. Remember you are praying to God and not the individuals listening. Keeping this at the forefront of my mind helps me to pray from a sincere heart. Sometimes I pray and I may misquote a scripture, mix up my tenses, or mispronounce a word. God is not concerned about that. He is not sitting in heaven going, "oh I can't answer that prayer because she said "is" instead of "are." Thinking too hard about how I "sound" and making sure I say the right phrases causes me to miss the true purpose of prayer. My prayer then becomes a performance instead of a sincere offering. Yes, others are listening as I pray out loud but I am not

focused on how they will grade my prayer. I am more interested in moving the heart of God. So take a deep breath and relax. Don't be anxious, just let your words flow from your heart. This is your daddy you are talking to, no need to be afraid.

4. Close your eyes. When I close my eyes especially when praying in front of others this helps me tune everyone out and focus in on God. When my eyes are closed, it helps me to get in a prayer zone.

5. Don't hold back. Don't worry about looking composed when praying in front of others. Real prayer requires vulnerability. If the tears flow as you pour out your heart, let them flow. Sometimes I am praying out loud and I am determined not to get loud and before I know it, my volume goes from 2 to 15. I am learning to be ok with that, just as long as it is not a work of the flesh. Do not censor every word that comes out of your mouth. Make room for God to use you prophetically as you pray. I have gone into prayer with a "script" in mind and then I feel God leading me to pray something else. I used to struggle with going off "script" because it was so uncomfortable to lose control when praying in front of others. I have prayed before and felt God leading me to pray something that seem to have nothing to do with the subject at hand. However, when I am done, I have had people come and say I prayed exactly what they needed to hear. Corporate prayer is meant to edify the one who is praying and the listeners, so pray as the spirit of God leads you without reservation.

Scripture for Meditation:

Matthew 18:19-20 (NIV)

Again, truly I tell you that if two of you on earth agree about anything they ask for, it will be done for them by my Father in heaven. For where two or three gather in my name, there am I with them.

Prayer Starter:

God, please help me get over whatever fear may be there when praying in front of others. Help me realize that my prayers can prove to be a blessing to others...

Reflection Questions:

Do you struggle with praying in front of others? If so, why?

Which of the pointers above stood out the most to you? Why?

Prayer is My Superpower

I do not wear a cape and I cannot fly or leap over tall buildings, but I have another superpower...PRAYER!

Jesus is my superhero and I consider myself to be His sidekick. Sidekicks typically have little or no power. However, in Luke 10:19, Jesus lets me know that I have power over the enemy and in John 14:12, He tells me that I will be able to do the same powerful works He did and even greater!

According to John 3:16 when I believe in Jesus, I am promised eternal life. Now *that's* superpower!

I am in a war with unseen forces, but I am not ill-equipped. With prayer I can stop the works of darkness, speak against generational curses and break them; I can change the course of my life! I can speak life to dead situations. Don't believe me? Ask the prophet Elisha who prayed for the Shunamite's dead son in 2 Kings 4. The Lord answered his prayers, and the boy was brought back to life. That is a superpower!

I can pray for Jesus to heal the sick. Don't believe me? Ask the woman in Luke 8 who constantly bled for 12 years. She spent all of her money going to doctors but they could not heal her. However, in an instant, healing was hers after touching the hem of Jesus' garment. I also have my personal testimonies from my last two children: Isaiah and Faith. They were both in need of healing; Faith had multiple diagnoses, including a heart defect and a possibility of a chromosomal abnormality. Isaiah had to have 3 surgeries in his first year of life because of issues with his small intestines and heart. We prayed and Jesus answered and healed them. That is a superpower!

Prayer, coupled with praise, can free us from the prison the devil tries to put us in. Don't believe me? Ask Paul and Silas. They did not complain or hold a pity party when they were in prison for the sake of Christ in Acts 16. They PRAYED and PRAISED which broke their chains and set them free! That is a superpower!

Prayer allows me to transcend my natural circumstance and enter a state of contentment and true joy. I never have to worry about anything. When I pray according to the will of God, I have an overflow of confidence because I know He hears and will answer me, and I can have joy in any situation. Don't believe me? Ask the Apostle Paul who wrote the words from Philippians 4:4 when in prison," Rejoice in the Lord always. Again I will say, rejoice!" (NKJV)

If all the above examples are not "super" enough. In prayer, the one who created the universe, speaks to me! He tells me His heart and His will. Don't believe me? Ask Abraham. The sins of

Sodom and Gomorrah were great and in Genesis 18 God shared His intentions to destroy these cities with Abraham. In this dialogue, God gives Abraham the opportunity to intercede for Lot and his family to be saved from destruction and they were. That is a superpower!
As believers, we have the power of prayer. Let us use it!

Practical Ways to Make Prayer A Priority

Congratulations! You made it through the 40 days! I pray you are encouraged to pray even more. Below are a few pointers to make prayer a priority.

Practical Ways to Make Prayer A Priority

- Schedule a time to pray, don't just wait for it to happen.

    o   I encourage you to set some time aside each day to pray. Set an alarm or put it on your schedule until it becomes a habit.

    o   If you are saying you don't have time to pray, take an inventory of what you do with your time. Make note of what takes up most of your time, is it always what is necessary?

- Remember, prayer is a conversation between you and God and should not be one-sided. After you share your heart with Him, sit still so He can share His heart with you. Often, we are more interested in what *we* have to say and forget that God's response to us is necessary. We pray and ask Him to tell us His will, but we don't sit still long enough to hear it. Obsession with hearing our own voice in prayer can hinder us from hearing the very answer we seek.

    o   Initially, sitting in silence may feel awkward, but the more you "practice," the more listening will become a habit.

    o   When possible, have a journal and pen on hand to write down what God is saying.

- Don't cancel your prayer by consuming spiritual junk after praying.

  - o Spiritual junk is anything that does not edify. What are you taking in for entertainment, what movies and television shows do you watch, what do you listen to? Also consider the company you keep and the conversations you have.

  - o God wants us to have times of refreshing, but beware that our recreation is not counterproductive.

- Keep a prayer journal

  - o Refer to day 38 for more details about how I do my prayer journal if you need an example.

- Don't be locked into one way of praying.

  - o Prayer is dynamic, be open to how God will lead you when you are praying. It may not look the same every day. Prayer is not about following a set formula but more about flowing with the Spirit of God.

- Don't wait for perfect conditions to pray.

  - o Life doesn't stop so we can pray, but we pray to ensure that life's circumstances does not stop us. For example, you may have young children in the home. You don't have to wait until they are all sleeping or doing a specific task before you begin to pray. Perfect will never happen, but that certainly does not hinder God from hearing your prayers.

Finally, I want to remind you again that prayer is not a performance. Remember it is your heavenly father you are speaking to. He delights in hearing from you, so get comfortable in His presence and pray on!

Anika's Other Book:

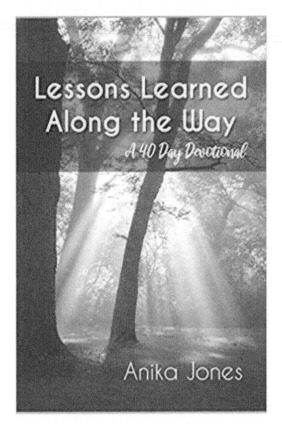

(ISBN # 1792641273,111 pages)

Lessons Learned Along The Way: A 40 Day Devotional

Lessons Learned takes you through 40 inspiring lessons about how God shapes and molds us during the different seasons of life. Each entertaining and thought-provoking lesson includes scriptures to meditate on as well as questions to sweep through the heart of where God is leading you.

Made in the USA
Monee, IL
23 August 2023

41487059R00111